The Darrell Royal Story

Darrell Royal (signature)

(Photo by Ike Baruch)   (Photo by Linda Kaye)

(Photo by Linda Kaye)   (Photo by Linda Kaye)

The Darrell Royal Story

Jimmy Banks

EAKIN PRESS ★ Austin, Texas

REVISED EDITION 1994

Copyright © 1973
By Jimmy Banks

Published in the United States of America
By Eakin Press
A Division of Sunbelt Media, Inc.
P.O. Drawer 90159, Austin, TX 78709

Library of Congress Card Catalog No. 73-86926

ISBN 0-89015-981-5

To my wonderful wife, Mary Virginia—

who is also known as "Dit" and

"Bussey" and as an angel

ACKNOWLEDGMENTS

Without the cooperation of Darrell and Edith Royal, gathering the material for this book would have been an impossible task. I am deeply grateful for their help and especially for their patient endurance of many, many hours of interviews.

I also appreciate the splendid assistance of Jones Ramsey, sports information director at the University of Texas-Austin; Wilbur Evans, executive vice president and general manager of the Cotton Bowl; Bob Hartley, sports information director at Mississippi State University; Allan Shivers, former governor of Texas; Mike Quinn, assistant to the chancellor of The University of Texas; the Rev. Fred Bomar, pastor of St. Peter The Apostle Church in Austin; and to all the Longhorn football players who have been so cooperative in interviews with me during the Royal years at Texas, but especially to Gene Bledsoe and Marvin Kubin.

And for the eloquent phrases I've borrowed from them, my thanks go to Dan Cook of the *San Antonio Express-News*; the late Walter Stewart, *Memphis Commercial-Appeal*; Norris Anderson, *Miami Daily News*; Melvin Durslag, *Los Angeles Herald-Examiner*; Emmett Watson, *Seattle Post-Intelligencer*; Royal Brougham, *Seattle Post-Intelligencer*; Jim Brooke, *Edmonton Journal*; Carlos Conde, *The Daily Texan*, and Lou Maysel, *Austin American-Statesman*, the author of a splendid history on University of Texas football.

The artist, Bob Grigsby, joins me in expressing appreciation to James Laughead, a great photographer, for making the fine picture which was used as the basis for our cover illustration.

—Jimmy Banks

CONTENTS

Chapter 1

THREAT TO THE THRONE

An undercurrent of tension electrified the strange, eerie silence of the Texas Longhorns' locker room. Despite the presence of Charley Pride and Willie Nelson, a pair of kings in the country-western music business, the place seemed as lively as a tomb. With the 1973 Cotton Bowl Classic only moments away, even the normal clacking of hard cleats on concrete was missing. The players' rubber-cleated shoes, designed for the artificial turf on which Texas was about to meet Alabama's Crimson Tide in one of the most dramatic games of Coach Darrell Royal's fantastic career, produced nothing but silence on the dark blue carpet.

Conversation was almost non-existent. The big, burly football players acted almost as if they were strangers, perhaps thrown together in some remote, isolated bus station. When they did speak, they used muffled tones—as if they didn't want to disturb the reverie of their teammates. Mostly, they just sat on hard benches and straight chairs, staring vacantly into space.

Outside, another sellout throng was beginning to jam the Cotton Bowl for the Longhorns' record-shattering, fifth straight appearance as the Southwest Conference's host team in the annual New Year's Day spectacular at Dallas. Many of the fans who had greeted 1973 with great enthusiasm the night before undoubtedly felt the 1 p.m. kickoff came painfully early but, to the Longhorns, it began to seem overdue by mid-morning.

The hour before the game was a long, long 60 minutes. Most of the players dressed quickly after arriving in the locker room. Occasionally, one of the coaches would confer briefly with one of them but, for the most part, there was nothing to do but wait. Many of the Longhorns sat and thumbed through the souvenir programs which had been placed at each locker . . . .

The front cover of the colorful booklet showed Cartoonist Bill McClanahan's likeness of a smiling Paul "Bear" Bryant, the Alabama coach, riding the crest of the Crimson Tide over a brick wall. McClanahan depicted Royal using two fingers to plug a couple of holes in the dike—and being backed up by the cartoonist's version of a Longhorn steer named Bevo, the UT mascot.

This seemed quite appropriate for a game in which Alabama, with only a freakish loss to Auburn staining its record, was ranked fourth in the nation while Royal's Longhorns, beaten only by Oklahoma, were ranked fifth. The gamblers rated Alabama a one-touchdown favorite.

Inside, the program's first article carried the byline of Jones Ramsey, Royal's sports information director for the previous twelve years. Before moving to the University of Texas, Ramsey had served Bryant in a similar capacity at Texas A&M for four years and had named his son, Paul, after Bryant. The article compared Bryant and Royal under the headline, "*I Wish My Son Could Play for Both of Them.*"

Ramsey had high praise for both men—and he noted that his feelings were shared by their contemporaries since "they're the only two men ever to be honored twice as Coach of the Year" by the American Football Coaches Association . . . .

Despite the lack of activity and noise in the locker room, the tension mounted steadily as kickoff time neared. The nerve-wracking suspense was compounded when an assistant came in to tell Royal "they're running about ten minutes late" and to keep his squad inside an extra ten minutes.

A page in the program, calling attention to Royal's having won or shared the Southwest Conference championship for five straight years, noted:

"One more trip to the Cotton Bowl Classic on Jan. 1, 1974, and the Texas coaching staff will have lapped the field. This marks the ninth year that Darrell Royal-coached Texas teams have played in the Classic; no other institution, through all coaching regimes, has played in the New Year's Day game more than five times.

"And just as nine appearances here represent a strong record, so does Texas' achievement of five straight Cotton Bowl trips. No other school has made more than two straight appearances.

"Texas' record during Royal's career there stands at 135 victories, 33 defeats and four ties, plus national championship teams in 1963, 1969 and 1970 . . . ."

In 16 years at Texas, Royal had won more Southwest Conference games—87—than any other coach in history; the previous record of 86 had been constructed by Jess Neely during 27 years at Rice.

At an early age, Royal had been crowned as one of the kings of college football—but powerful Alabama now posed a strong new threat to his throne. Three times before, Royal had sent a Texas team against one coached by Bryant, one of his longtime football idols. Royal's teams had won two of those games and the other, in the 1960 Bluebonnet Bowl, ended in a tie; Bryant, obviously, would be pulling out all the stops in an effort to defeat his young friend for the first time.

While the crowd outside watched the pomp and pageantry in bright sunshine, Royal dressed for the cold rain expected to hit during the game. He spoke briefly to some of his special guests—Dr. Stephen Spurr, president of the University of Texas at Austin, and Spurr's son, Dan; Marty Jurow, the movie producer who had become fascinated with University of Texas football while working on a movie about Freddie Steinmark, the courageous cancer victim; and his old friends, Pride and Nelson.

Royal finally sat down in the small cubbyhole which served as a dressing room for the host team's coaches. He took off his baseball cap and, for a few moments, buried his head in his hands.

An innocent bystander might have thought he was trying to collect his thoughts and perhaps decide what to tell his squad before sending it out to face Alabama—especially since the Longhorns had lost the 1972 Cotton Bowl game to Penn State, 30-6, and the 1971 Classic to Notre Dame, 24-11.

But Royal insists that none of his pregame remarks are premeditated —and that even in this situation he was not composing a pep talk. Instead, he said, he was "just thinking about a little bit of everything—and nothing in particular . . . ."

The kaleidoscope of thoughts flitting through his mind included a great many questions: *Have we worked the squad hard enough for this game? Or too hard? Is President Johnson here yet? Man, I'll be ready for that vacation with him next month. Will that rain hold off until the game's over? Maybe the weatherman's wrong—again. Wonder what David's doing—and Mack, and Marian, and the grandkids. We really need to win this one. Recruiting. If we lose, they'll be saying we choke in the big ones. We've gotta win this one . . . .*

Royal had spoiled Longhorn fans to such an extent that those two straight Cotton Bowl losses had caused some grumbling among the orange-blooded die-hards. There was nothing serious about it—except to Royal. The friendly, blue-eyed Irishman with the engaging smile does not really cotton to criticism, especially when he feels it is not justified.

Earlier that week, he shrugged off mild—but stinging—complaints from a few football fanatics about the players' being permitted to arrange their own transportation to Dallas again, just as they had done for those ill-fated 1971 and 1972 Cotton Bowl games. Royal authorized this because the Cotton Bowl Classic came during the middle of the students' Christmas vacation and most of the players wanted to return to their homes immediately after the game, instead of going back to the campus at Austin.

"Maybe you should keep them together—fly them up there," was the essence of some of the free and unwanted advice he received.

This irritated Royal considerably. He felt that it made no difference at all whether the Longhorns went to Dallas individually or as a group, especially since they stayed together there from the time they arrived Friday night until after Monday's game.

"People tend to forget that you've gone to the Cotton Bowl five straight times," he declared, "and to remember that you've lost two straight there."

That was merely one of many reasons Royal wanted so badly to beat Alabama; there were some other unusual circumstances involved.

He was still smarting from an Associated Press series of five articles, published six weeks earlier, which implied that he was a "racist"— although nothing could be further from the truth. And a book by a former Longhorn football squadman had just appeared, blasting college football in general and Royal's brand of it in particular.

Most fans paid little attention either to the AP series or the book. It really was not the Texas fans who were *demanding* that Royal win this one; it was Royal himself.

Darrell Royal was already a living legend in the football world, although just 30 years earlier he had been a skinny, freckle-faced high school football player in Hollis, Oklahoma, supporting himself by shining shoes. And that shoe-shining job was one he had "worked up to" after several grubbier, lower-paying ones.

He had never, since grade school, wanted to be anything but a football coach. To most people, achieving that goal would have seemed impossible when he fled the Oklahoma "Dust Bowl" with his family in 1940 to pick fruit in California, at 10 cents an hour. That escapade climaxed a miserable childhood for Royal and, after an especially unpleasant spat with his stepmother, with whom he never got along, he hitchhiked back to Oklahoma—where he finished high school and went on to win All-America fame at the University of Oklahoma.

His life has been stalked by so much tragedy and graced with so much glory that even Horatio Alger would have been laughed out of the park had he tried to detail it as a fictional story. The true facts, far stranger than fiction, include two automobile mishaps which almost killed him before his rise to the pinnacle of football success. And they are laced liberally with shocking paradoxes.

Now a gifted, widely-sought public speaker, Royal almost quit coaching during his first year in the profession because he "drew a blank" and had to sit down without delivering one word of a scheduled speech at a high school banquet in North Carolina. But part of his record-smashing success generally is attributed now to his superb speaking ability. And his homey witticisms, especially since he took the Texas coaching job in 1957, have intrigued the nation's "sophisticated" sportswriters almost as completely as his innovations—such as the "Flip-Flop" offense and the "Wishbone T" formation—have fascinated both friend and foe.

Royal, an avid country-western music fan, blazed a new trail through the nation's sports pages with such expressions as these:

We're gonna dance with who brung us!
A kid who looks like he needs worm medicine....

*There ain't a hoss that can't be rode and there ain't a man that can't
be throwed.*
*Playing Texas A&M is like opening boxes of Crackerjacks—there's a
surprise in every package ....*
*They're like cockroaches—it's not what they eat and tote off, it's what
they fall into and mess up that hurts ....*

Among those captivated by the Royal mystique was President
Lyndon B. Johnson. After leaving the presidency, Johnson played golf
frequently with Royal and saw practically all the Longhorns' football
games—including the thriller with Alabama, which came just three weeks
before his death.

Not long before that fateful New Year's Day game, Johnson
confessed to a group of dinner guests: "I'm really not much of a football
fan; I'm a fan of human beings. And I'm a great fan of Darrell Royal,
because he is the rarest of human beings ...."

Royal was a Lyndon Johnson fan, and his friendship with the
President had a tremendous impact on his life. Among other things, it
triggered a keen interest in political affairs—and there was a time when
some of Royal's closest friends even suggested seriously that he run for
governor of Texas.

On Jan. 1, 1973, however, Royal's friendships with the high and the
mighty—and even his own fame—seemed far away as he waited
impatiently for the test that was about to take place before the crowd in
the Cotton Bowl and many millions of television fans.

Suddenly, without any warning or prompting, All-America Tackle
Jerry Sisemore—a mammoth man, 6 feet 4 inches tall and weighing 265
pounds—jumped up from his chair in the locker room and began making
a speech. Emotion obviously tried to cram the words back down into his
huge throat but they kept gushing forth, repetitiously and without much
order, in the only "pep talk" of his career.

"We've got a choice to make," he declared, almost sobbing. "It's up
to us .... I don't know about you—but this game, it means a lot to me.
We'll have a long time to remember it. It's my last one .... We've got a
choice to make and it's up to us ...."

He finally summed up what he had been trying to say in one climactic
sentence: *"Let's whip their ass!"*

His teammates listened as if they were in a trance. Later, most of them
probably could not remember what he had said but they would never
forget that he helped them get "ready" or "psyched up"—something
which the blunt, outspoken Royal believes is essential in the brutal,
"unnatural" game of football. A game, incidentally, which he does *not*
contend builds character.

As soon as Sisemore sat down, Royal got up.

"I want each of you," he told his players, "to promise yourself that you'll go all out on every play, with every ounce of energy you've got, regardless of the score or the amount of time left to play. I don't care whether it's the first minute or the tenth minute or the fifty-ninth minute; I want you to put everything you've got into every play.

"You might be able to fool the guy next to you, or even the rest of your teammates, but you can't fool yourself. That's why I want you to make that commitment to yourself, not to anyone else.

"You seniors have had three Conference championships," said Royal. "There aren't many people walking around in Texas who can say they've played on three championship teams. But we still don't have a bowl victory—and we need one real bad.

"If you'll go all out on every play, we can beat this bunch. They're not going to put out that kind of effort—because they don't think it's necessary. They think they can beat us without it. They'll put out a good effort—but they won't be fanatical . . . ."

It wasn't much like the movies, partly because Royal's "pep talk" was interrupted by an assistant's calm, business-like announcement that "it's time to go out."

"Okay," said Royal, matter-of-factly, "let's go."

And then, suddenly, it *was* like the movies—with the huge, orange-and-white-clad Longhorns crowding toward the door, their motors obviously running, as they cried to each other, "Let's go!" and "Let's get 'em!"

It was the kind of enthusiasm which such expert generators as Willie Nelson and Charley Pride dream of generating . . .

Fate wasted little time in flipping the Longhorns a curve. They received the opening kickoff and, on the third play from scrimmage, Quarterback Alan Lowry threw a pass. Alabama Safety Steve Wade intercepted at midfield and a few moments later Greg Gantt kicked a 50-yard field goal, the longest in Cotton Bowl history, to give the Crimson Tide a 3-0 lead with the game less than four minutes old.

And that was just the start of a dismal first half for Texas.

Three minutes later, Longhorn Fullback Roosevelt Leaks—a 205-pound, sophomore battering ram who had gained 1,099 yards during the regular season, averaging 4.8 yards per carry—was knocked into the next day. He wandered over to the sideline and Dr. Paul Trickett, the team physician, immediately began checking him over. Dr. Trickett quickly determined that Leaks was not seriously hurt—although he had a slight case of amnesia. That is quite common in such cases and Dr. Trickett gave him a few whiffs of an ammonia-scented towel.

Royal, now the business executive striding back and forth on the sideline, paused to check on Leaks' condition. Then he turned quickly back to the action on the field. He wore a headset with attached microphone, communicating constantly with Assistant Coaches Freddy

Akers and Willie Zapalac in the pressbox as he made his decisions on which plays to call.

Four plays after Leaks went out, Lowry tried a long pass to Halfback Tommy Landry (no relation to the Dallas Cowboys' coach). Wade thought it was Christmas all over again as he intercepted on the 'Bama 27 and returned to the Texas 31. On the next play, Halfback Wilbur Jackson scampered 31 yards for a touchdown. Bill Davis' extra point kick made it Alabama 10, Texas 0, with almost five minutes left to play in the first quarter.

Texas fans began to fear that a rout might be in the making.

Leaks returned to action and Texas launched a 71-yard drive that finally stalled at the Alabama 8. Leaks carried five times for 32 of those 71 yards. On fourth down, Billy Schott, a sophomore who set a school record by kicking 28 extra points in 28 tries during the regular season, booted a 24-yard field goal—cutting the Alabama lead to 10-3.

Later in the second quarter, the Longhorns drove from their own 40 to the Alabama 15. Leaks contributed a 10-yard gain on one play and then made seven, to the 'Bama 37, on the next one—but got hurt on that one and left the game again. Schott tried a 32-yard field goal, with one minute and 41 seconds left to play in the first half, but it was wide to the right and the Tide took over on its own 20.

Quarterback Terry Davis responded with a furious aerial assault, completing four straight passes for a total of 54 yards. With just eight seconds left on the clock, Bill Davis kicked a 30-yard field goal that made it Alabama 13, Texas 3, at halftime.

Royal, who felt his players had been mentally ready for the game, sized them up quickly during the intermission and became worried over their obvious dejection. Deep gloom saturated the locker room and the Longhorns were so quiet that Royal feared they had given up.

Akers and Zapalac showed Royal, on a blackboard in the coaches' dressing room, how Alabama's defensive halfbacks were playing Texas' split receiver to the outside consistently, even when he faked inside. They agreed he could probably get open by running a post pattern—turning inside and angling toward the goal posts instead of cutting outside.

They told Lowry and the receivers to change that pattern but, so far as strategy was concerned, that was the only halftime change.

Meanwhile, Dr. Trickett and Trainer Frank Medina were working with Leaks. In response to questions, Leaks couldn't remember his assignments—or much of anything else.

Again, the wait seemed interminable. As the time finally neared for the second-half kickoff, Royal turned and asked Leaks, "What do you do on 28?"

Leaks, slumped in a chair, looked up, shook his head slightly and mumbled, "I don't know."

Royal shook his own head and turned away. He felt certain that

Texas could not possibly win without Leaks rampaging through the line.

Zapalac decided it was time to head back for the pressbox and looked around for Akers. He found him talking to Lowry, who was seated among a bunch of players sitting in chairs and glumly contemplating the blue carpet.

Zapalac walked over to Akers, touched his arm and said, "Let's go."

Suddenly, it was almost as if he had ignited a volcano. A low rumble began among the few players who had heard him, then spread almost instantly, with explosive intensity, throughout the room. The Longhorns erupted toward the door, with determined looks and low-pitched exclamations of intent which made them seem as blood-thirsty as a lynch mob.

"WAIT!" yelled Zapalac, throwing both arms over his head and motioning with his hands for them to sit down again. "It's not time for *you* to go out!"

The players settled back down, not realizing that they had just told Royal what he wanted to know.

"I'd been worried because they were so quiet," Royal said later, "and then it dawned on me that they'd really been boiling inside."

Once again, he called them all together in one end of the long locker room. He talked to them for only a few moments, in the reassuring manner of a kindly father reminding a crestfallen son of the rewards that can be gained through patience, persistence and hard work.

"We didn't do so bad the first half," he declared, "except for failing to score twice when we got down there close. Just keep it up, playing the way your're playing. If you do, we'll get *us* a pass interception, or a fumble...."

It was, of course, more of a hope than a promise.

On the sideline, after Texas kicked off to Alabama, Royal called Dr. Trickett aside.

"How about Rosey?" he asked. "Can he play?"

"Well, yes," the doctor replied, "but he may have trouble remembering his plays."

"I'm not worried about that," Royal responded. "I just want to know this: medically, is it safe to play him?"

"Sure," said Dr. Trickett, "it's perfectly safe—"

"Okay, then. I don't want anyone giving him any more quizzes on what day it is or what his assignments are. I'll take care of that."

Royal then found Leaks.

"Rosey, we don't have a Chinaman's chance in this ball game with you sitting on the bench," he said. "We can't win it without your help. Do you think you can handle your assignments?"

"I don't know," said Leaks.

"Well, get out there and do the best you can," said Royal. "If you can't remember what you're supposed to do, just guess—and try to head in the right direction."

On the Longhorns' first play from scrimmage in the second half, Leaks ripped through the middle for three yards. That initiated a 59-yard, 15-play touchdown drive on which Leaks carried nine times for 37 yards. Lowry sprinted around the left side for the last three yards and Schott's extra point kick made it Alabama 13, Texas 10, with 4:43 left to play in the third quarter.

The Longhorns clearly were back in the ball game now, and their fans began to go wild with anticipation.

Midway through the fourth quarter, Texas' Terry Melancon, a second-string sophomore, intercepted his second pass of the day—this one in the end zone for a touchback that prevented a touchdown.

Eighty yards to go. Seven minutes and 42 seconds left on the clock. Three points behind. Now or never. Do or die.

The first try was a highly un-Royal type of play. Jim Moore went daringly deep on an end-around and was lucky to get out with a one-yard gain.

Second down and nine. Lowry hits Pat Kelly with a 20-yard pass. Then Leaks blasts the middle for one yard. Second and nine, again. Lowry passes to End Julius Whittier for 16 yards and a first down on the Alabama 42. Then Lowry keeps at the right side for two yards. Second and eight. Lowry fakes to Leaks, then hands off to Donald Ealey for a gain of six.

Now it's third and two, from the Alabama 34. Four minutes and 33 seconds left to play. On the sideline, Royal recalls Lowry's suggestion a few plays earlier that a risky bootleg play they had used only once all season looked ripe. Royal confers briefly on his headset phone with Akers.

"If we're ever going to use it, it might as well be now," says Royal. "It may be time to go for a bundle."

Lowry takes the ball, starts to his left and once again fakes to Leaks crashing into left guard. Then he fakes to Landry, slamming at left tackle—and hides the ball behind his own left hip, drifting a few yards deep to reinforce the illusion that he has given it away. It works perfectly. The Tide defense pulverizes Leaks and Landry—but here is Lowry, all alone in left field. He dances down the sideline and is almost forced out—or is he?—at the 11-yard line by a Tide defender. But Lowry stays on his feet and sprints into the end zone.

Schott kicks the extra point and it's Texas 17, Alabama 13, with 4:22 left to play.

For years, they'll talk about Lowry's brilliant 34-yard touchdown run. The telecasters run it back on instant replay time after time, insisting Lowry stepped on the sideline at the 11. Some newspaper photos purportedly show that he did, although prudent editors note that camera angles can be deceiving. Anyway, all this matters not. Jerry Stephens, the official trailing Lowry down the sideline, insists he was always in bounds and that's the way it goes into the records.

But the final score does not go into the record book just yet. There are still four minutes and 22 seconds left to play between two of the best college football teams in the nation.

After the kickoff, Alabama launches a drive from its own 10, into the teeth of a ferocious Texas defense led by Randy Braband. In seven plays, the Tide manages to reach the Texas 43. Now comes another moment of truth. It's fourth down and one, with 1:40 left on the clock. Alabama desperately needs just one yard for a new lease on life.

Jackson smashes at right tackle—and is smashed right back by Braband, with a jarring tackle that makes him *lose* a yard!

Now, suddenly, the Texas bench breaks into bedlam. The players go wild. Even Dr. Trickett, a small, dignified man with a mustache, jumps about three feet off the ground, clapping his hands, grinning from ear to ear and shouting, "We did it! We did it!"

It is, some of the Longhorns testify later, the first time they've ever seen him show any emotion at all.

Texas decides to stall out the remaining 1:36—but almost scores again, anyway. Another 34-yard run by Lowry takes the ball to the Alabama 11 but there he is content to run out the clock—for one of the greatest victories of Royal's almost unbelievable career.

In the locker room once again, Royal called his players together briefly before admitting the sportswriters. His advice was short—and, of course, sweet.

"Let's remember that the Alabama players have been fine sports. They didn't do any popping off before the game. They've been gentlemen—and let's be the same. I don't mean that you have to subdue your smiles," he said, breaking into a big one.

"Personally," he added, raising both arms again and clenching both fists in the "Hook 'em" sign, "I intend to do a lot of smiling!"

Nearly everyone except Royal, Pride and the latter's two young sons, Craig and Dion, had left the locker room more than an hour later when Edith Royal came in and congratulated her husband.

Royal finished dressing quickly—although he spent several minutes looking for a missing sock.

"Now, what in the world could have happened to *one* sock?" he asked. "If somebody put it on by mistake, he must have left another one here . . . ."

He couldn't find another one, however, and wound up putting one of his shoes on a bare foot.

Two Cotton Bowl cars with drivers waited outside for the Royals and their special guests for the game. In addition to Mr. and Mrs. Pride and their two sons and Mr. and Mrs. Nelson, these included Mr. and Mrs. Joe Jamail of Houston and Dr. and Mrs. Harold Stinson of Tuscaloosa,

Alabama. Dr. Stinson was president of Stillman College, a Negro school which Royal had been serving for three years as a member of its board of trustees.

All were going to the Royals' hotel suite for his favorite kind of celebration: an informal "picking" session with Pride and Nelson passing the guitar back and forth.

"We can all get in these two cars," Royal assured them, "if you don't mind crowding up a little and sittin' in laps."

A cold, dreary darkness was falling over the Cotton Bowl as they all piled into the cars but, in the private world of Darrell Royal, the sun was shining as brightly as it ever had.

Someone had asked him before the game if going to the Cotton Bowl wasn't getting a little monotonous after five straight trips.

"No," he replied. "The only thing I can think of that's better than five—is six."

After Air Force service during World War II, Royal became an All-America quarterback at the University of Oklahoma.

Chapter 2

"OKIE"

Contrary to widespread belief, Darrell K. Royal's middle name is not "Kenneth." As a matter of fact, he doesn't even have a middle name. His middle initial was given to him in honor of his mother, Katy Royal, and the fact that it has no literal meaning seems ironically appropriate because her death, while he was an infant, left a great void in his life.

Darrell grew up thinking that his mother had died while giving him birth, on July 6, 1924. That tormenting thought haunted him throughout his youth, simply because "cancer" was an unspeakable word in those days—one which his elders refused to face. He did not learn the true cause of his mother's death, nor even the fact that it occurred four months after he was born, until he was grown.

His father, Burley Ray Royal, a native of Montague County, Texas, had moved to Hollis, Oklahoma, in 1918. He worked there as a bookkeeper, a truck driver for an oil company and, for a brief time, as a jailer and deputy sheriff. When his first wife died, he and their six children—four sons (Ray, Don, Glenn and Darrell) and two daughters (Mahota and Ruby)—moved in with his parents, who also lived in Hollis.

There were plenty of people around to take care of little Darrell—all but the one he needed most.

"The main thing I remember about my early years, before I became interested in athletics, was the fact that I didn't have a mother," he recalls. "I guess any kid that doesn't have a mother goes through the same thing. I wanted a mother very much. I used to daydream a lot about what it would be like to have a mother . . . .

"I had a lot of relatives in my home town. I got all the love and attention that a child could ask for. But I guess no one can replace a mother, regardless of how much they love you and care for you and look after you."

In addition to love and attention, Darrell also got all the teasing that might be expected from five older brothers and sisters. His father recalls coming home from work one day to find Darrell, then about five years old, lying on the front porch, kicking and screaming and "throwing an honest-to-goodness tantrum."

"I found out later that one of the girls had hidden his ball," said

Burley Royal. "He just let his temper get the best of him. He was raising all kinds of cane. I lifted him real good for that and, as far as I know, nothing like that ever happened again."

The elder Royal was driving a kerosene truck about that time and young Darrell's innate curiosity led to one of his most pungent childhood memories.

"I crawled up on top of that truck one time," said Darrell, "and there was a big metal lid up there with two arms you twisted to get it off. I managed to get that lid off, and then I stuck my head down in there to look around. I hollered—and there was really some echo. I was intrigued with the sound. I stayed up there and sang a few songs. I kept smelling those gas fumes—and I got sicker than hell. I mean *really* sick. So sick that gasoline fumes and that kind of stuff still bother me."

Although he can still recall those nauseous fumes without half trying, that miserable misadventure now seems only a trivial part of the grief which haunted Darrell's early life.

About the same time that Burley Royal built a new house and remarried, when Darrell was six years old, Ruby died suddenly of food poisoning. Then, four years later, Mahota, the oldest of the Royal children, also died suddenly and unexpectedly, of a heart ailment. Darrell was playing touch football out in the street when one of his older brothers came to tell him about Mahota's death, bringing him face to face with tragedy.

"I don't really remember Ruby," said Royal, "but when Mahota died, it really shook me up."

It shook up the entire Royal family, physically as well as emotionally. Mahota's husband, Claude White, and their two children, Barbara and Bobby, moved into the crowded Royal household. And this happened just as the Great Depression was tightening its grip on the throat of America. Millions of people searched hungrily for jobs that didn't exist. In Oklahoma, the problem was compounded by a gargantuan drouth which turned much of the Midwest into murderous clouds of choking, wind-whipped dust.

At night, Darrell and other members of his family slept with wet rags over their faces in an attempt to filter the dust. During the day, he and his brothers spent most of their spare time playing football—using a tin can for a ball. Darrell recalls that it always "was a 'Clabber Girl Baking Powder' can—because that was the only one we could find that was just the right size."

Don Royal, who later became a highly successful coach at Tipton (Oklahoma) High School, remembers those days vividly.

"We used to get out there with the other kids on the block," he said, "and play 'pass and tag' with one of those tin cans. Darrell and Glenn [the third oldest] both got to where they could throw it pretty good."

Glenn later became baseball coach at Altus (Oklahoma) Junior College.

"No one had any money in those days," noted Don. "But finally, all four of the Royal brothers went in together and bought a rubber football for a dollar and fifty cents. You could get a pretty good one for that then. It would probably cost twelve or thirteen dollars now. But we were so careful with that ball for a long time that kicking was strictly against the rules because we were afraid we'd bust it."

Darrell's share of the investment came from his paper route. He *ran* that route, literally—and almost from the time he became old enough to walk.

"I used to have to tie a knot in that paper bag to keep it from sagging down below my knees," he said. "Bicycle? Man, I couldn't afford one. Tennis shoes were my bicycle. I'd fold those Hollis papers and hit 'em on the run. It used to be a big thing to hit the door with it and holler, 'Paper!' And you'd be surprised at how many people would come right on out and get the paper; they'd be just sitting there waiting for it.

"I ran just because I liked to. I never went any place across town that I didn't run. I don't think I ever walked to school; I'd hit it on the run. I used to run every place I went. I remember I used to go see Grandma Royal; she lived out at the north edge of town. It would be in the summer and I'd get ready to go home. You know, as a little kid, you wanted to go see your grandma and grandpa but you didn't want to stay all day. But she'd fuss about me leaving in the heat of the day and say I ought to wait until it got cooler.

"I used to walk from her house real slow until I got out of sight—and then take out running. But I didn't want her to see me running because I knew if she did she'd make me stay 'til sundown."

There were a few times when Darrell wished he had been walking instead of running. Once, during the dead of winter, with a cold north wind battering his face, he was running at top speed across the school playground when a big iron ring, hanging from a chain on a gym set, struck him squarely in the mouth. The heavy ring broke off one of his front teeth. The damage was repaired at the time with a gold cap but then, while he was playing service football during World War II, he took another hard lick on the same tooth. An Army doctor pulled what was left of it and replaced it with a bridge—which, unfortunately, got separated from Darrell a few times while he was playing for the University of Oklahoma.

He could have saved himself a lot of misery by sidestepping that iron ring the same way he sidestepped shrubbery and trees while running his paper route.

"I turned that paper route into a sort of a game, I guess the way I did nearly everything else," he recalled. "I'd fold that paper so I could throw it good and then try to hit certain spots with it.

"Some of my customers were blacks who lived in the alleys," said Royal. "Sometimes, they wouldn't have the money to pay me and they'd say, 'I'll catch you next week.' I'd always let the paper run. It cost a dime a week and I got a nickel of that. Sometimes they'd get up as high as thirty or forty cents but they'd always wind up paying me."

The young businessman wanted a bicycle very badly but realized that, even without losing any money on bad debts, "you couldn't buy one on a nickel a week a customer."

"The only bicycle I ever had in those days was one that belonged to my brother, Ray," he said. "He was a mechanic and somebody came through there and sold him one. He bought it just because it was such a good price.

"Man, I rode the wheels off that bicycle—until he got a chance to sell it at a profit. I remember how sick I was when he did sell it. The only one I ever owned was one I bought when I was a freshman at Oklahoma. I used to ride it to and from classes. But I caught a ride home with one of the other football players one night and left it on the campus and somebody stole it. You never chained 'em up in those days but it was really unusual to have one stolen."

Darrell kept his paper route until the *Hollis Daily News* switched from daily to weekly publication. When that happened, he got a job feeding the press all night long, one night a week, for 25 cents an hour. That was one chore even *his* active imagination could not tie in with some phase of football but at least it was one which didn't necessitate his out-running stray dogs.

"When I was running that paper route, some of those dogs made me a little more light-footed," he remembers. "I used to pet dogs all the time. That was a weakness of mine. All of 'em didn't want to be petted, I found out, but any kind of pet, I'd want to stop and pet it.

"Now that I'm older, I really don't want to touch a dog or a cat. And I especially don't want anything to do with them when I'm inside a house. I guess this is kind of a quirk of mine but I can't wait until I get in and wash my hands after I've touched 'em. I love dogs and I love animals but I just want to go wash my hands after touching them—and I sure don't want them around where I'm eating."

Perhaps because dust filled the Oklahoma air so frequently during his childhood, Royal has a fetish about clean hands. It is not uncommon for him to wash his hands 15 or 20 times a day; after he reads a newspaper, for example, he cannot wait to wash the ink off his hands. And while he was growing up in Hollis, dogs stayed outside the houses; for one thing, most of the houses, especially in his neighborhood, were too crowded to have dogs underfoot.

Darrell discovered early the thrill of competition and, when he couldn't find other people to compete against, he competed against himself or even tried to out-run dogs and cars. But, sometimes, competition took place in the cotton fields and wasn't the least bit fun.

"We didn't pick cotton—we pulled bolls," he declared. "The cotton in Southwest Oklahoma wasn't good enough to pick; it was stunted, because of the drouth. So you'd have to take the boll and all. You'd hook your fingers on the stalk and run 'em to the boll and snap it off—taking the boll, cotton and all.

"We used to go out real early in the morning but whoever owned the field wouldn't let you start pulling if there was any dew at all, because that'd make the cotton weigh more. They made you wait until the sun really had it parched and bone dry before they'd turn you loose. Seems like we'd always have to wait a coupla hours. I can still smell those green cotton leaves. And it's not a good smell to me because it reminds me of something so unpleasant.

"It was always real hot out there. We'd take our drinking water in a Mason jar and put it in the shade of the wagon where we dumped our cotton. It seemed like the sun would always change so that when you wanted a drink, that water would be in the sun and be real hot. And, as hard as you'd try, you couldn't keep dirt from getting in the bottom of the jar—so when you'd drink it, you'd have to be real careful not to stir up that dirt in the bottom of the jar.

"We used sacks nine and a half feet long. My sack would usually have eighty or ninety pounds in it when I weighed in. I'd pick about four hundred pounds, maybe sometimes five hundred, in a day. And we were getting two-bits a hundred.

"One thing's for sure: pulling those bolls sure made you want to go to school."

Darrell wore cotton gloves but the needle-like burrs still attacked his hands and made them sore. Somehow, they bothered him a lot more than the "goatheads" he collected every day during recess and after school, when he always seemed to be the ringleader in games involving frequent contact with the ground. And the ground in Hollis was covered with goatheads—sticker burrs which each had two long, punishing prongs capable of causing real misery. As a result, Darrell kept a safety pin stuck in the bib of his overalls. He spent much of his classroom time using that safety pin to dig the goathead barbs out of his hands, knees and feet.

He collected quite a few of those while playing a game called "Join."

"I'd be captain of one team and some other guy would be captain of the other," Darrell recalls. "We'd run around the playground and jump on some guy and wrestle him down. If you could get him down and make him say 'Join,' then he'd be on your side and he'd help you go around and force others to join your team. And if a guy was too tough for one guy to handle, two or three would jump on him.

"Seems like I always played something that got my clothes torn up. And when you knocked the knee out of your overalls, that always made a big hit when you'd go home."

Still, Darrell invariably would find some game to play on the way home from school, then brace himself for the punishment he knew was coming. He found that, in sports, it didn't matter where you lived or what you wore if you could score touchdowns or hit the basket consistently or pitch well . . . .

"We used to have a weekly baseball game between the kids on the east side of Hollis and those on the west side," said Royal. "I was about twelve or thirteen years old, I guess, and I used to pitch. We'd go over before every game to Wilcy Moore's house. He had been a relief pitcher with the New York Yankees. He had a catcher's mitt and mask he'd let us borrow every week.

"I did a lot to keep those games going for a coupla years, because they really meant a lot to me. And my team usually won. I remember once, I was out visiting an aunt of mine who lived in the sandhills northwest of Hollis. I was about to miss that game, and had planned to miss it. But then, at the last minute, I decided I just couldn't, and I walked the six or seven miles into town to play in it.

"When I first learned to throw a curve—and it was just a kind of a roundhouse thing—I tried to curve it on every pitch. When I could first see it curve a little, I'd throw it and then ask the catcher to tell me if it had curved. I always wanted 'em to say 'yes' so bad, but it seemed like they'd always say, 'Nope, couldn't see anything on that one.'"

Meanwhile, however, Darrell had devised various means for measuring his progress in other sports endeavors. He used an old wheel from a toy wagon for a discus and hurled it consistently from the same place, driving stakes in the ground to mark his longest throw. Then he found a ditch containing powder-like dirt, and decided it was ideal for a broad jump pit; he'd jump and mark his distance, then come back the next day and try to beat it. He would also run along the edge of the highway and, when he saw a car, pick out a fence post or a sign and try to out-run the car to it.

But it was much more fun, he found, to compete against people.

"Every guy that moved to town, I had to test," he recalls. "It was something I just felt we had to get settled. I'd size him up and finally get him in a tackle football game or a wrestling match. And I'd usually win— not necessarily because I was so tough but, I suppose, just because I'd stay with it more.

"When I was in the sixth grade, I started doing a little boxing. A guy named Jess Woodman, who had done some amateur boxing and was pretty good, had a body repair shop there and he used to teach the kids a little about boxing. And he'd fight all the carnival guys that came through town, asking for volunteers to box 'em.

"One of the first fights I ever had was over in a little town called Arnett. We'd get up a team and go over to these other towns and enter local tournaments. Well, the guy I was supposed to box that night didn't show up. So they asked if there was anybody else there in my weight division that wanted to box me.

"There was a guy there from Dodson, Texas, who was a distant cousin of mine and whose name also was Darrell Royal, and he volunteered. He was about four years older than I was. He'd been coming into Hollis on Saturday nights and kinda bullying me around, and I was really pretty scared of him. My Dad was there that night and they asked him if it was all right for me to fight this guy. He said he didn't have any objections if I didn't.

"Well, I did—but I wasn't about to admit it. I really thought I was going to get whipped bad and I didn't want any part of it. But there wasn't anything I could do but go through with it.

"When that guy got in the ring, he grabbed the ropes in the corner and did a few knee bends, glaring at me over his shoulder, just like a real pro. But as it turned out, that was about all he could do. He couldn't fight a lick and I whipped him real bad. After that, I could walk the streets of Hollis on Saturday night and he'd give me plenty of room. And that was one worry I didn't have anymore.

"It taught me that over-respect for your opponent can be just as dangerous as under-respect—and that you shouldn't let people bluff you just by putting on a big show."

Later, while he was in high school, Darrell's limitations as a boxer came home to him quite forcefully. He entered the Golden Gloves Tournament at Altus and, in his first bout, lost a decision.

"I just ran out of gas," he says of the defeat, "and it really surprised me. I thought I was in superb condition—and I was, for things like football and basketball. But I just wasn't properly trained to go really all-out in a fast-paced fight for three rounds. Boy, it really did embarrass me, to have to go back to school the next day after getting ironed out. But that's good for everybody once in a while, to get put down."

While he suffered his full share of "put-downs" during his youth, few of them were in sports; he excelled in nearly every one he tried, with the exception of boxing. And, because of his natural curiosity, he tried just about all of them. That curiosity still shows up frequently, as it did the time he met a ventriloquist in Houston and spent an hour questioning him on the art of throwing his voice.

Darrell's rapt attention finally prompted the ventriloquist to ask, "Is this guy putting me on?"

Royal was only 12 years old in 1936, when President Franklin D. Roosevelt made a whistle-stop campaign appearance in Childress, Texas, 30 miles southwest of Hollis. Darrell slipped away and hitchhiked to Childress for the occasion.

"The thing I remember most about it," he says, "was weaving my way around all those legs of grownups and working my way up next to the railroad car to see the President. That—and the fact that I was afraid to tell my folks what I'd done.''

He hitchhiked back to Hollis and feared the worst when the man who stopped and gave him a ride turned out to be Joe Horton, a close friend of his father's. But the incident escaped notice until Darrell confessed, many years later.

"I was afraid to tell anybody—but at least I'd gotten to see my President," Royal recalled.

It probably was curiosity, as much as anything else, which prompted Darrell to start hanging around the high school football practice field when he was still in grade school. He listened intently to Coach Jake Spann and his assistant, Dean Wild, explain blocking and tackling and passing and punting techniques. And then he'd go off and practice those techniques by himself.

"I used to idolize those guys on the high school team, and especially those on college teams," says Royal. "We'd play in the yard on Saturdays, when I was a little kid, and we'd put the radio on the porch and turn it to the broadcasts of the Oklahoma games. The band would play 'Boomer Sooner' and, in my mind, I was on the Oklahoma team—and that band was playing for *me*."

By the time he reached junior high school, Darrell was spending much of his classroom time drawing X's and O's—trying to diagram football plays. And daydreaming about coaching.

"When I was just a little older than they were, I used to want to coach little kids—who really weren't even ready to play football," he said. "I wanted to organize 'em into a team and get somebody else to organize another team, but I couldn't get anyone else interested—not even the little kids."

He found that less frustrating, however, than the fact that he could not get other boys his own age to take sandlot football games as seriously as he did. A fierce competitor with a raging desire to win, he couldn't understand others who "horsed around" and refused to "go all out" on the sandlots.

His fiery competitive spirit earned quick admiration from Joe Bailey Metcalf, his junior high school football coach. Metcalf recalled that Royal, both in junior high and high school, would stay on the practice field as long as he could every day, practicing his punting after everyone else had gone. That was true, he noted, even during Darrell's high school days when he was going downtown every night to shine shoes.

"He worked about as much as any kid his age I ever saw," said Metcalf, "But he also found time for a lot of other things. He was a leader in everything—including the mischief."

Royal pleads *nolo contendere* to that charge. And, pressed for an example of the mischief, he recalls with a grin one of the nights when he and some of his friends went jackrabbit hunting.

"There was a guy on the staff at school that we really liked, and I don't know why we thought it was something to play pranks on him," said Royal. "But we went out in an alfalfa field one night and killed a bunch of jackrabbits, then threw 'em on his front porch.

"Well, in a little town like Hollis, it's got to be one of four or five or six guys that's responsible for something like that. How you gonna get by with that? Well, I didn't. And because of that, they made me miss one of our junior high school football games.

"And there was a guy named Calvin Philley—you know that with a name like 'Philley' his nickname would be 'Mare'—who was in our gang. He was more mischievous, if that's possible, than any of the rest of us and how they missed him, I don't know. But he got to play in that game and turned out to be the star runner. And to make matters worse, he was at *my* position. I sure didn't like that."

It was about that time that Darrell learned a lasting lesson from Metcalf, as a result of some mistake the youngster made on the football field. Royal has forgotten exactly what precipitated the brief lecture, and so has Metcalf, but Royal remembers his coach's words clearly: "Alibis, alibis, alibis! All I ever get from you is alibis!"

"Boy, did that embarrass me!" says Royal. "I started thinking right then that if you did it, it's obvious, and if you didn't deliver, that's obvious, too; so there's no use trying to alibi or cover it up."

At home, meanwhile, Darrell's stepmother did not give him many opportunities for alibis or explanations about what she felt were his misdeeds.

"When my grandpa on my mother's side, Grandpa Billy Harmon, died," said Royal, "That left my grandmother alone and she only lived a coupla blocks from our house. So I started spending the night with Grandma Harmon. I actually had my clothes and everything at home but, at night, I'd go stay with her."

The friction between Darrell and his stepmother made that arrangement much more attractive than it might have been under normal circumstances. But Darrell was so engrossed in sports by then that he wasted little time worrying over family relationships.

During the spring of 1940, just after Darrell finished junior high school, his father decided to join the mass exodus from the Dust Bowl to California.

"This was during the Depression, the Dust Bowl days," Darrell recalls painfully. "There was a long string of cars outside our house all the time, headed west. We were just a block from Highway 62 and they'd head out it and go to Midway, which was midway between Childress and Wellington. Then they'd go on up north and hit Highway 66 and join the Okies from the other part of the state on the way to California to pick fruit.

"My stepmother had a son who had gone to California and bought a little farm, near Porterville, so we headed out there.

"I hadn't thought much about being an Okie, in any way other than pride, until we hit that highway. You talk about typical Okies—Papa had an old Whippet automobile and he built a trailer. He put a load of furniture on that trailer, then sold the rest of the stuff and sold the house. And we took out in that Whippet and that was all of it, what was on the back of that trailer. That ol' Whippet would just barely make it through the mountains, especially on the inclines. We had some of those canvas bags tied on the side for our water. That was supposed to keep it cool but it didn't—that water was almost as hot as the sun. And flats, we must have had fifteen or twenty going out there.

"When we finally got to California, we got in the fruit harvest like everybody else. But we were living in an old shack. And pretty soon, I started noticing that I talked a lot different from the kids who'd been raised in California. I had that southwest twang—and I still do, to this day.

"It was a little bit of a show of weakness on my part but I started working hard to keep from talking like an Okie—because they could spot you at the snap of a finger. And it wasn't one of those things you could be proud of because 'Okie' then was really a dirty word. I guess it wouldn't be nearly as cutting as calling a black a 'nigger' but there is some comparison there, because they sure didn't mean it to be complimentary."

More than a quarter of a century later, Royal could look back and reflect: "There's something pretty unjust about things when a whole people are made to feel inferior when all they're trying to do is find enough honest work to live on."

The experience stamped itself indelibly on his mind, helping to shape a philosophy which would influence thousands of youngsters during his coaching career.

"I tried as fast as I could to start talking like a person from California," says Royal. "But I soon found that I didn't want any of that. I didn't want to live in California—not under those conditions."

That feeling was reinforced by a letter he received from Coach Wild, who had been promoted from assistant to head coach at Hollis High School, offering to get him a part-time job that would help feed and clothe him if he wanted to return to his home town and play football. As the summer dragged on in this strange state where everything seemed so different, the lure of Hollis became stronger and stronger.

"I guess what really capped it off," Royal recalls, "was a run-in I had with my stepmother. It was pretty bad. That night, I asked Papa if I could go back to Oklahoma—and he'd seen what happened—and he said I could.

"I had an old Victrola case that had been gutted—all the record-playing stuff had been taken out of it—and I used that for a suitcase. I put everything I owned in it—including my baseball glove, which I thought more of than the small amount of clothes or anything else I had. My Dad gave me about thirteen dollars and I started hitchhiking back to Hollis from Porterville.

"I caught a ride down to Bakersfield and when I got there, I remembered that a guy named Billington, from Hollis, owned a used-car lot on the highway circle. My Dad had pointed it out to me when we went through there on the way to Porterville. I stopped by there, just because Mr. Billington was from Hollis.

"I guess maybe he thought I was too young to be hitchhiking so he told me about this agency that would get you a ride for a small fee. We went down there and I paid ten dollars for a ride to Oklahoma.

"The man I rode with had a withered arm and he drove with one of those knobs they used to have on steering wheels," said Royal. "He was supposed to stay on Highway 66 and let me off at Shamrock, Texas. And we were driving straight on through, without stopping to spend the night anywhere.

"Well, everything went fine at first but then he got to nipping on a bottle. He was drinking it straight while we were driving along. We got off Highway 66 but he said everything was all right, that he had just decided to take the southern route. Well, we got close to El Paso and had a blowout, up on a mountain road—and I guess I'm within six inches of not being here. He was drunk and we weaved over on the shoulder of this road, up on a high cliff. He finally managed to stop the car, right on the edge. It was straight down and if we'd gone off, it was certain death.

"Of course, I was just a kid and I didn't have sense enough to leave that guy and catch me another ride. We finally got the tire fixed and I stayed with him. But then he changed his mind again about which way he was going. He said then he'd take me to Childress. But the way if finally ended up, he went to Abilene and that's where I left him.

"It was dark when I got out of his car so I headed straight for the courthouse. I figured that was the safest place to be, because the policemen and nightwatchmen operated out of there. My Dad had been a nightwatchman for a while and I've always felt friendly to law enforcement officers. I've always felt real good, and comfortable, when I've been around a policeman.

"When I got to the courthouse, I crawled up in the flowerbed next to the building, under some hedges, to get some sleep. I had on some real thick corduroy pants. It was real popular then, especially among the California kids, to wear corduroy pants and never wash 'em; the dirtier they were, the better. And I was wearing a real wide belt.

"I got up under those hedges and unfastened that belt, then looped it through the handle of that old Victrola case—like I had something in there that was just too valuable to leave lying there—and buckled myself

to it, so nobody could get it without waking me up. And then I went to
sleep."

Several hours later, during the middle of the night, Darrell awoke
suddenly—terrified by a bright light shining into his eyes and blotting out
the rest of the world.

Chapter 3

A WAR FOR ALL

Darrell grabbed instinctively for that treasured Victrola case as a gruff voice behind the bright light shining into his eyes demanded, "What are you doing there, boy?"

"I was just sleeping," replied the youngster.

"Well, come on outa there!"

Darrell crawled out from under the hedges, scooting the Victrola case along with him. Then he learned that the flashlight which had awakened him was being held by a policeman and he breathed a massive sigh of relief.

"I don't know how he'd found me there but he took me inside and started quizzing me," said Darrell. "I told him the whole story—how I was hitchhiking back home from California and everything. But at first he didn't believe me. He seemed to think I was running away from home or something.

"Then I remembered the letter from Coach Wild and I dug it out of that Victrola box. After the policeman read that, he believed me. He said, 'Well, you might as well sleep in here; we've got a cot we're not using.' I got on that cot and slept there the rest of the night. Of course, I could have slept anywhere after the trip from California. The next morning, the policeman fed me some breakfast and then I took off. I hitchhiked on back to Hollis that day."

Darrell's grandmother was delighted to see him—and so was Coach Wild, who quickly arranged a part-time job for him at Bill Hall's automobile dealership. Darrell reported for work every morning at 5 o'clock to sweep and mop the floor, then clean up the grease rack. After that, he would go home and change out of his greasy clothes in time for school. In addition, he washed cars on Saturdays; his total pay was $5 a week.

"Grandma Harmon was on an old-age pension and I gave her two dollars and fifty cents a week for what I ate there," Royal recalls. "Then I put two dollars a week into clothes. You'd be surprised at how quick you could get something paid for, at that time, at two bucks a week. Of course, I wasn't buying anything very expensive.

"That would leave me about fifty cents a week for breakfast. Coach

Wild lived right across the street from the school and he used to take me over to his house for lunch, so I was able to make it pretty good.

"I used to go right by Ward's Bakery every morning on the way to work and on real cold mornings, especially, those rolls and bread just coming out of the oven would really smell good. I'd usually buy a couple of rolls for my breakfast. I'd go in and get those hot rolls just coming off and then I had some milk I kept in the Coke box down at the motor company. I'd have a roll or two and some milk for breakfast nearly every day. Man, it really tasted good."

Darrell's healthy appetite and his natural ambition prompted him, after several months, to take on an additional job—as a short order cook and "bustin' suds" at Marvin Whited's Cafe, in return for all his meals. Then, later on, he discovered he could make more money shining shoes than he could handling both his other jobs simultaneously.

"Cecil Sumpter, one of the real good friends who helped me a lot, ran the barber shop," said Royal. "His son, Cecil, Jr., was shining shoes there and decided he wanted to quit so he started teaching me something about it."

Royal learned quickly, tackling the job with the same competitive spirit, inquisitiveness, determination and enthusiasm he displayed in everything else. He even scouted his competitors (all of whom happened to be black) and picked up some valuable tips from them.

"I used to go by and swap trade secrets with them—see what kind of polish they were using, how many coats they'd put on, what kind of shoe cleaner they used, what kind of sole dressing they used," he recalled. "I remember one of the old guys there—he'd been shining shoes for a long time—pointed out to me right quick that you really couldn't give a good shine, a good, clean glossy shine, with a dirty rag or a dirty brush. That polish gets in there and cakes up. It doesn't spread the polish as well and it gets kind of greasy, giving the shoes a dull look. You really need a clean rag to put a glossy shine on, so I used to wash my rags and brushes with soap and water.

"And it still bothers me when I get a shoe shine from someone who uses a dirty rag," said Royal, whose own shoes now are kept polished to a mirror-like gloss.

"I got ten cents for a shine and got to keep it all, in return for being janitor at the barber shop. I had to sweep up, and 'Bon Ami' the door and windows and mirror, and wash up everything, so I had my own key. I'd go down and open up on Sunday mornings because you could always pick up a few shines before church.

"The shop was right next to the theater. They usually had an evening show and, before it started, people would kinda congregate around there waiting for it to open. A lot of times, the high school band would even come down there and play in front of the show.

"So I'd hustle down there late in the afternoon from football, baseball or basketball practice—whatever I was playing at the time—and open up the shop. There would always be at least two or three guys that would come in for a shine and I could make enough that way to pay for the evening meal."

While young Darrell was delighted to find such lucrative jobs, he was sorely disappointed by a ruling that he was ineligible to play high school football in 1940, after returning from his first summer in California.

"They ruled I was ineligible although I had been born in Hollis, had gone to school there every day of my life and was sleeping in the same bed there I'd slept in ever since the seventh grade," he declared. "I didn't think it was fair, and I still don't think it was fair. But they had to adopt some rules to keep Texans from moving up there just to play football, since they had an age limit in Texas and we didn't. So they said you had to be living with your parents, or else lay out a year."

A familiar gleam lighted up Royal's blue eyes, as he recalled those days.

"Only I really didn't lay out the full season," he said, with a chuckle. "I played against Capitol Hill High School in Oklahoma City—which wasn't any pleasant experience, by the way. We got beat about forty-eight to nothing. We really got trounced around. I got to play because we had a guy named Bill Husband, who later became a doctor in Elk City, on our team and he was injured. So I took his uniform and played as 'Bill Husband' in that game.

"I played in another one, too, while I was ineligible, and it was really an unusual experience. We went over to the Federal Reformatory at Granite and played the prison team there, inside the walls. They even fed us there—we went in and ate in their chow hall. This was just a rake-up team of local guys but they were afraid I'd be declared ineligible again for the next season, if anybody found out about it, so I played under an assumed name.

"They had a guy in there who was a life termer, whose name was Big Ed, and he was their fullback. I remember that I was very much impressed with Big Ed.

"Later they came to Hollis for a return game. They played on the local field and there were armed guards all around it. But if one of the prisoners had broken and tried to run away, the guards couldn't have shot because there were so many people there.

"I didn't play in that game because people would have recognized me and it might have cost me my eligibility. But I watched it, and it was on a cold night. We built a fire down there, from scrap lumber left when the WPA built the dressing rooms. We'd warm up around that fire under the grandstand, then go out and watch, then come back and warm up again."

Darrell worked out with the high school team, the Hollis Tigers, all that season, chomping at the bit in his desire to play. It was a long, long

school year and when it finally ended, he decided to go back to California
for the summer with his brother, Glenn.

"We got out there and got hold of an old Model T Ford and
overhauled it so we could drive it home," he remembers. "It didn't have a
top and that sun out in the desert on the way back really got hot. But it
rained on us coming through the desert and that really felt good.

"We'd drive until we got tired, then pull off the road behind a
billboard and go to sleep. Then, when we woke up, we'd take off again.
We never did buy any oil. The service stations, when they'd drain oil out
of cars, would put it in drums. We'd pull up and get 'em to give us some of
that oil they'd drained out of other cars.

"But still, we finally ran out of money and gas at the same time—just
as we pulled into Hollis. We'd used the last money we had to buy gas in
Amarillo."

By then, Darrell was more than ready to get back to football—and
C.L. "Dick" Highfill, who had replaced Wild as the Tigers' head coach,
was delighted to see him. Although he only weighed about 124 pounds,
Royal became the regular tailback—and signal-caller—in Highfill's
double wing offense during that fall of 1941.

Darrell's fierce pride took quite a beating that season, as the Tigers
won only three games. But Highfill, who sometimes suited up and
scrimmaged with his team, was building for the future—and he could see
in Royal the potential of a leader as well as strong triple-threat
capabilities.

Highfill took Darrell to see his first college football game that year, an
Oklahoma game at Norman that was played in the rain. The main thing
Darrell remembers about it was the great punting of Indian Jack Jacobs.
He carefully studied the way Jacobs dropped the ball when he was
punting—then went back home and changed his own style, trying to
emulate the great Oklahoma kicker during his endless hours of practice.

Darrell seemed to find some time to "mess around" with a football
almost every day of the year, even while he was lettering in basketball and
baseball. For him, even the coldest north wind that ravaged the prairies
around Hollis never made it too cold to practice punting. But there were
many times when he was walking home from basketball games late at
night, sometimes with cardboard in his shoes to cover up the holes, when
he thought he would freeze.

"Grandma Harmon was really something, and she'd always wait up
for me," he recalls. "We'd go out of town to play a basketball game and
ride that old bus, that didn't have a heater in it, back to the school after
the game. Then, by the time I'd walk home, my hands and feet would
really be cold. I'd knock on the door and she'd always ask, 'Who is it?'
That was just automatic. And I'd say, 'It's Darrell.' Then she'd say,
'Lord, nobody could mimic that voice—I'd know it if I heard it in
France.' That was just automatic, every time I'd come in late.

"And then, when I'd get in bed, I'd find that she had heated one of those old flatirons for me. She'd wrap it in newspapers and then in a towel, and then put a blanket around it and put it in the foot of my bed. Boy, that would feel good! You'd get in that feather bed and put your feet on that, then snuggle down and you could really sleep.

"Of course, as a young, healthy kid without any cares or worries, I never did have any trouble sleeping, anyway . . . ."

By the time the 1942 football season arrived, Royal's fiery, competitive spirit almost seemed contagious on a Hollis Tiger squad which included Don Fox, Glenn Whisenant, Leon Manley (who later became one of Royal's assistant coaches at Texas), Clinton Cunningham, Bill Covin, Leroy Whitman, Cecil Sumpter and Abb Sheid.

Royal scored four touchdowns as Hollis swamped Elk City, 59-0. The next week, Hollis met Hobart, then rated second in the state, in a downpour of rain and Royal sparked the Tigers to a 13-0 victory.

Then came the big one—against powerful Classen High School on its home field, in Oklahoma City. Classen was heavily favored but Royal threw two touchdown passes, then intercepted a pass and returned it 60 yards for a touchdown as Hollis scored a stunning, 27-14 upset.

It was Royal who was stunned, however, after the game when University of Oklahoma scouts who had been watching it came to the Tiger dressing room.

"They talked to three other guys and didn't talk to me and, boy, I really had my feelings hurt," he said. "I was deflated, dejected and really just crushed. Of course, it's understandable that they were not interested in me because I just weighed about one forty-five and didn't have a whole lot of speed.

"But," he added, "I didn't know I was small . . . ."

Royal scored one touchdown and passed for the other in Hollis' next game, a 13-0 win from Altus. In fact, he played a key role in each of the Tigers' eight victories that fall. They won another game on a forfeit and finished undefeated.

That was before they had state playoffs in Oklahoma and Enid also ended the season undefeated. Coach Highfill challenged Enid to a game, and when Enid rejected the invitation, Hollis claimed the state championship.

"Coach Highfill said we were state champions and that was good enough for us," said Royal.

Royal's running, passing and punting had earned him first team All-State honors—and finally attracted the attention of the University of Oklahoma, which offered him the football scholarship he had wanted so badly for so many years.

His exploits also earned him increased respect from a young lady named Edith Thomason, who lived on a farm near Gould, about 20 miles from Hollis. In fact, they turned her into an avid football fan although she had never seen a game before that season.

"I first met Edith in the summer of '42," said Royal. "She was in town visiting a girl friend of hers, one of my classmates that my brother, Glenn, had been dating. The girls had gone to the movie and a bunch of us were hanging around the soda shop when they came out. We got to talking to them and Glenn and I walked them home."

Darrell and Edith promptly began dating—and her father, A.M. Thomason, must have wondered about his daughter's sudden interest in football that fall. She managed to talk him into driving her back to Hollis, despite the handicaps of wartime gasoline and tire rationing, for several of the Tigers' games that season.

The next spring, not long before his class was scheduled to graduate, Darrell volunteered for the draft.

"I quit going to class because, in those days, if you were drafted while you were in your last semester of high school, they automatically gave you your diploma," he said. "I knew I was going in so I just quit going to school. You know, kids were kinda unsettled about that time—and I wasn't all that fired up about school work, anyway.

"But then I took the physical—and flunked it. Because of a football injury, I had water on the knee. So, all of a sudden, there I am, rejected by the draft and not going to class. And I really needed that diploma so I could get into college eventually. I went back to school and, fortunately, some understanding people there let me pick up where I'd left off so I could graduate.

"I took another physical in July and passed it, then went right on into the Army Air Corps."

It was a far different ball game then, so far as military service was concerned, from the one which would later confront many of his players at the University of Texas.

Shortly before the Vietnam cease-fire agreement was announced, Royal looked back and compared the attitudes of his contemporaries during World War II with those of the young men drafted for service in the Southeast Asia conflict.

"When I volunteered for the draft," he said, "all three of my brothers already were in the service. A lot of guys were volunteering. All of us agreed that we should; there wasn't any doubt about it. Things weren't going just real good for us in the war. And this was a war every one of us knew we were in—it was a war for all. There was full agreement we should be in it. We had no choice but to be in it.

"But I can imagine how these young kids feel now, when our top politicians can't decide whether we ought to fight harder or pull out of Vietnam completely. I just can't think of anything that would be more frustrating to a young kid than to have to fight under those circumstances.

"My decision wasn't hard because everyone agreed that we had no choice. I can't say that I really looked forward to going, or that I was anxious to go," he added. "For one thing, I was love-sick at the time . . . ."

On a warm July evening in 1943, Darrell borrowed the car that belonged to the wife of his brother, Ray, who was in the service, for a date he had with Edith Thomason. He still remembers the white dress with dark blue polka dots she wore that night, on the eve of his departure for active duty at Fort Sill, Oklahoma. They parked on a lonely country road, beneath a big Oklahoma moon, and talked about the future.

For the first time, they talked about the possibility of getting married some day. Time has obscured most of the details, except for those polka dots, but this is the way Darrell recalls the incident now: "It was kinda like, when this is all over, let's tie the knot. And she said she was gonna be there when I got back."

It was a young Royal family that moved to Austin. Left to right are Marian, David, Edith, Mack and Darrell.

Chapter 4

STRANGE WORLD OF KHAKI

Darrell woke up early the next morning, long before the alarm clock went off, and started getting ready to catch the bus to Lawton. Grandma Harmon was up about the time he was, fixing his breakfast and reminding him to "be sure and write."

The 100-mile trip took what seemed to be an eternity. Darrell fidgeted in his seat, looking out at the bleak Oklahoma countryside and wondering what would happen when he reached Fort Sill—and if he would ever come this way again.

A cold, drab Army bus met the new recruits in Lawton. It was commanded by a tough-sounding sergeant who obviously wanted everyone to know that this was war; he treated the inductees almost as if he were taking them prisoner.

The next few days were filled with physical and mental exams, psychological and aptitude tests, needles in arms, the issuance of uniforms, countless roll calls and the incessant nagging of drill instructors trying to teach this group of civilians how to march. Royal took the aviation cadet exams, although he had never been in an airplane, "just because that seemed the glamorous thing to do."

He spent only a few days at Fort Sill.

"It was long enough," he recalls, "to learn how lonesome that ol' bugle sounds when they tell you to turn out the lights and go to sleep, and you realize you're a long way from home . . . ."

As it turned out, the Army Air Corps had all the aviation cadets it wanted, at that point, but aerial gunners were in great demand; as a result, most of the "Wild Blue Yonder" applicants were assigned to gunnery school. But first, they had to take basic training. Darrell was sent to Miami Beach for that.

"Our 'barracks' there was the Kent Hotel," said Darrell, "and at the time, I thought it was really something. But I went back and looked at it when we went down there for the 1965 Orange Bowl Game and it hadn't seemed to hold up very well."

About the time Darrell's class finished basic training, all its records were lost—and the entire group had to go through "basic" again. This turned out to be the first in a series of unusual Army incidents which were to have a great impact on his life.

"I was young enough and strong enough that going through basic a second time really didn't bother me," he said. "We had a basketball there and a hoop down on the parking lot outside our hotel, so I used to spend a lot of my spare time down there shooting baskets—with a guy named Jerry Araino, a lot of the time.

"The first time I ever heard the 'Aggie War Hymn' was in Miami Beach. We had a guy down there named Bernard Ott, who had been a freshman at Texas A&M. We always sang something while we were marching and he got us to singing that. Man, I didn't know what I was saying when I sang, 'Good-by to Texas University.'

"We used to go over to Flamingo Park and play touch football. One night, in the hotel, I started to go downstairs and just as I got almost to the lobby, I heard some of our drill instructors down there talking. One of them had seen me playing touch that afternoon and I heard him say he thought I really had a future in college football.

"I went back to my room—but I didn't sleep that night, I was so excited. And I figured that guy must really be a football expert."

Darrell still was figuring out ways to compete, almost every minute. Once, during a drill field break, he enticed another trainee into a contest to see how far they could throw their dummy hand grenades. Instead of lobbing them in the prescribed manner, Darrell threw them the same way he threw a baseball, and just as hard—until a first lieutenant he didn't even know came over and stopped him.

"Soldier," said the big, tall, muscular-looking lieutenant, "do you have any serious interest in athletics?"

"Yes, sir," Royal responded instantly.

"Then quit trying to throw your arm away," he said. "You can ruin it that way."

Royal went from Miami Beach to the gunnery school at Harlingen, Texas, where he took his first airplane ride. It was in an AT-6, a two-place pilot trainer with plexiglass canopies covering the cockpits.

"They strapped us into those parachutes, and showed us how to use 'em and everything before we went up," he said, years later. "So you know the main thing I remember about my first airplane flight? I had an urge to jump. I just kept thinking about all they'd told us about how to bail out in case of emergency, and I wondered what it would be like . . . ."

He didn't really mind the flying in aerial gunnery school (although he always was subject to motion sickness) as much as he did the shooting.

"I didn't enjoy any part of shooting guns," he admits. "Some of those guys used to love to shoot skeet, and couldn't wait until we'd go out to the skeet range. But I couldn't wait until my shotgun shells were all gone. I still don't care about shooting a gun. And I've never shot a deer, although

I've been on quite a few deer hunts. I have shot some coyotes and bobcats, mostly from a helicopter, and that was fun."

Most of his shooting at Harlingen was from turrets in B-24s. The gunners, each using different colored bullets which left their own distinctive marks, fired at target sleeves pulled by other airplanes. Royal did well enough at that to win his silver aerial gunner's wings. In the best shine-boy tradition, he promptly bought some polish and spent quite a bit of time shining up those new wings before wearing them proudly back to Hollis on his first furlough.

Edith was waiting, just as she had promised, but she was still in high school and they both knew it was far too early to "tie the knot." When he left again, this time for Davis-Monthan Air Base at Tucson, Arizona, she renewed her promise and said she would still be waiting . . . .

At Davis-Monthan, Darrell was assigned to a flight crew as tail gunner on a B-24.

"That thing sure flopped around a lot, and it seemed like we were always at the back of the formation, where we got all the propwash," he recalls. "It was really cold at 24,000 feet and your breath would freeze in those old oxygen masks. Seemed like those masks had a real funny smell, kinda musty-like. And you could smell all those gasoline fumes coming back at you. It reminded me of that time I got up on Papa's kerosene truck. I'd feel pretty queasy after every flight."

Of the 60 crews which completed heavy bombardment training at Davis-Monthan in the spring of 1944, Royal's was one of the three picked for photo reconnaissance training—at Will Rogers Field, just outside Oklahoma City. The other 57 went overseas.

That was about the time Edith Thomason graduated from Gould High School. She promptly moved to Oklahoma City, where she shared an apartment with two of her former high school girl friends, and got a job at Tinker Field, another army base.

"I was mending flight suits there—those heavy, leather suits with lamb's wool lining—after people got shot out of them," she said. "We'd fix 'em up just like new."

"Yeah," said Darrell, "after she told me about that, I started inspecting mine to see if it had been used before . . . ."

The First Methodist Church was only two blocks from the apartment where Edith lived. Omar Ross, another gunner on Royal's crew, and his girl friend accompanied Darrell and Edith when they got married there on July 26, 1944.

"We went up and knocked on the preacher's door, and we had the license, so he married us," said Darrell. "I'd just gotten a furlough so we went ahead and got married and then went back to Hollis, on the bus, and said, 'Here we are.' It's lasted so long it makes you wonder what's the right way to go about getting married, and at what age . . . ."

Darrell was 20 and Edith 19.

When Darrell reported back from his furlough, his crew was reassigned to weather reconnaissance training—also at Will Rogers Field.

That gave Sergeant Royal an opportunity to star in the Post Touch Football League. He led the 655th Bombers to three consecutive victories in their first three games before he was thrown for a loss by appendicitis.

"I jumped off a porch there one morning and felt a sharp little pain in my stomach," said Darrell. "I didn't think it was anything serious but I went on sick call, anyway. They slapped me in the hospital and jerked my appendix out, before they even called Edith to tell her I was sick."

By the time he got back on his feet, Darrell's flight crew had finished training, picked up another tail gunner and gone overseas. He began hanging around the post gymnasium while he was recuperating and, before long, he became a starter on the Will Rogers Field Eagles' basketball team. He quickly moved into the spotlight along with a couple of former college stars, Frank Mack (now a New York lawyer, and the man for whom Darrell names his oldest son) and Ed Milkovich.

He also won the respect and admiration of Captain Chester Friedland, who was in charge of physical training at Will Rogers; in the long run, that proved highly important.

During the spring of 1945, shortly after Royal switched from basketball to baseball, Friedland contacted some of his friends at Third Air Force Headquarters. He had a talented young man who he felt should get a tryout for the Third Air Force football team, he told them.

"They asked him about my weight and experience, of course," said Royal. "He had to tell 'em I weighed about one fifty-five and only played in high school. They had nothing but college football players so they thought this was kind of absurd. But they did agree to give me a tryout."

That was in April of 1945. Edith, expecting their first child within three months, went with him to Tampa, Florida, where they lived with Mrs. Sulu Beddingfield, a friend of one of Darrell's Hollis friends. They were living with her when Marian was born. Later, the Royals moved into a one-room "deficiency" apartment, with a bed that folded into the wall and a lavatory in one corner. It turned out to be a poor place for such chores as washing diapers.

Meanwhile, Darrell had been "lost" and then "found" at Drew Field. When he first reported for duty there, he was placed in a "personnel pool" which supplied talent for such sophisticated chores as "kitchen police" duty and mowing lawns. But then he went out for the baseball team—and got assigned to help build a baseball diamond.

One of those assigned to help was a German prisoner of war, whom Royal knew only as "Otto."

"He spoke practically no English and I spoke absolutely no German," said Royal, "but we learned to communicate pretty good. He didn't smoke but I used to buy candy bars and give to him. Sometimes I'd even give him a couple of extras to take to the other guys. Through sign

Frank Broyles, O. J. Simpson and Royal enjoy a laugh at a football banquet in 1983.

language and what talking we could do, we agreed that I had no desire to kill Otto and he had no desire to kill me. And we really became pretty good friends, considering our problems in communication and the fact that he was a prisoner of our Army.

"Some people thought it was dead wrong for me to give candy bars to those Germans but I couldn't see anything bad about it, and still don't. I never could understand it but some of the guys on our side really did have hate . . . ."

Royal reserved his "hate" for his opposition on the football field. And he had plenty of admiration for some of his own teammates, most of whom had been college stars before entering the service. They included, for instance, such All-America heroes as Charley Trippi from the University of Georgia and Bill Swiacki of Holy Cross, along with Joe Eddins of Auburn and Ted Cook of Alabama.

Although Royal was about the only one who had no college experience, he was not awed enough to think he would have any trouble making the squad.

"I could just look around and see some of those guys that couldn't run and couldn't catch and didn't want to hit anything," he said. "And I could tell that, unless they had a helluva lot of 'em hid out somewhere else, I was gonna make it."

Early in September, financial problems and the difficulties of living in a one-room apartment with a little baby prompted the Royals to decide that Edith and Marian should return to Oklahoma. Darrell moved into a barracks reserved for the Third Air Force football team, which also had its own mess hall—and nothing to do but play football.

"They even brought the payroll around for us to sign and then brought us our money," said Darrell. "As a matter of fact, I was a staff sergeant for a long time before I found out about it, because we didn't have to report to anybody but the football coach."

The coach was Maj. Quinn Decker, a disciple of Gen. Bob Neyland at the University of Tennessee—whose system was to have a profound influence on Royal.

The War ended in August but Darrell knew he had a long time to wait before getting discharged—and he felt he was really lucky to be able to play football while he was waiting.

"I'd have stayed in for that season even if I'd had a choice, just to play football," he said, "because it was too late for me to play in college that season. And after being out of football for two years, I was really anxious to get into it."

Bob Andridge, who had played at the University of Tennessee, became one of Royal's closest friends—and his best tutor. The two of them spent a lot of time together in the barracks, talking about defensive halfback play, and many long hours on the practice field with Andridge demonstrating what he had been talking about in the barracks. Royal still credits Andridge with having taught him "more basic techniques about defensive secondary play" than anyone else he has ever encountered.

"That season had a tremendous impact on my career, especially in regard to the footwork for a defensive back," said Royal. "I worked on all those techniques and drills constantly. And I used them at the University of Oklahoma, although they weren't teaching them there. I guess Andridge worked on my head as much as my feet, but I was a great student for him because I enjoyed hanging around the barracks and talking about football."

He also enjoyed playing it, of course, but one of the more remarkable things about his career as a player was the fact that he actually enjoyed practicing, even twice a day.

"I was one of those nuts who enjoyed spring practice," he explains. "I even looked forward to two-a-days. I just liked to play and liked to train and liked to try to make the team. Oh, I can't say I honestly enjoyed two-a-days while I was out on the field—but I looked forward to it, and anticipated it, and didn't dread it, like most players did."

At Drew Field, it was all football for Royal during that fall of 1945—and he loved practically every minute of it. He started the season substituting for Trippi at fullback and for Bob Kennedy, an All-America from Washington State, at wingback. Early in the season, Trippi was discharged (amid charges political influence had been used to get him back into a Georgia uniform, which created quite a furor). Kennedy then went to fullback and Royal began playing regularly at wingback.

But Royal didn't wait until Trippi left to get the attention of Third Air Force football fans. In the season opener against the Army Air Force Personnel Distribution Command, on Sept. 23, 1945, he returned a punt 55 yards for a touchdown.

It felt good to be back in a football uniform, especially in this strange world of khaki. But there was something eerie and unreal about it, almost dreamlike. Darrell could hardly believe his own ears when a public address announcer would introduce the Third Air Force players before a game and sounds such as these rolled across the stadium:

"Charley Trippi, All-America back from the University of Georgia . . . Cass Myslinski, All-America center from West Point . . . Bob Kennedy, All-America back from Washington State . . . Darrell Royal, a back from Hollis, Oklahoma, High School . . . ."

By the time the Third Air Force met the Army Air Force Training Command Skymasters in the seventh game of the season, Sgt. Darrell Royal had attracted the attention of college recruiters throughout the country. It was indeed fortunate for him that he had—because he suffered a broken wrist during that 7-7 tie with the Skymasters and was sidelined for the rest of the season. He already had shown enough talent to have a great many colleges courting him, especially since freshmen were eligible to play varsity football then and he had four years of eligibility.

He still was a member of the Third Air Force team when it went to Los Angeles for its season finale against the First Air Force in early December. From there, the footballers were given furloughs which enabled them to return home for Christmas.

After spending the holidays with his family in Oklahoma, Darrell returned to Drew Field—only to find that most of it had been closed up.

"The office we were supposed to report to was gone," he recalled. "I had all my stuff in my B-4 bag, and no place to go. I just couldn't find anybody to report to. But then I found out we were supposed to report in at MacDill Field, across town, and they had some of those GI buses to take us over there.

"Just as I was leaving, I ran into Otto. I hadn't seen him in quite a while, and I visited with him as long as I could. He'd learned to speak a little more English, too, by then. I told him it looked like I was getting out of the service, and I had the feeling he really was happy for me. But I'll never forget how sorry I felt for him when I pulled out of that gate on the GI bus. He didn't know if any of his family was alive, or when he'd be released, or anything . . . ."

Royal had a cast on his arm when he was discharged, and the small bone in his wrist which was broken bothered him for more than a year. But he was so glad to get out of the Army that he paid little attention to that minor inconvenience, even though it caused him to miss spring practice at the University of Oklahoma in 1946.

Among the many colleges which had tried unsuccessfully to lure him away from the school of his childhood dreams were the Citadel (where Quinn Decker had become head coach), Florida, Alabama, USC, Texas Tech, Georgia, South Carolina, Tennessee, Cornell, Auburn and the University of Detroit.

This was in the days before the National Collegiate Athletic Association began policing college football, and some of the schools seemed to be working overtime in demonstrating the necessity for such a move. All was fair in love and peace, so far as many of the colleges were concerned, and they had plenty of "rah-rah" ex-students who were more than anxious to subsidize exceptional football talent.

Royal's talents were most exceptional—and, naturally, he received a number of outstanding monetary offers. As a man with a wife and child, just out of the Army and entering college, he studied them carefully. Several were highly tempting but he knew he wanted to attend the University of Oklahoma, and perhaps hear that band play for him in reality the way it had played "Boomer Sooner" for him in his childhood fantasies . . . .

He kept getting pressure from other schools throughout the country but no encouraging words from OU—although it had offered the customary room, board, tuition and books scholarship.

Finally, Darrell talked the situation over with Edith and they decided that, since he really wanted to attend OU, they could struggle along on the standard scholarship even though he did have a wife and a baby to support. He would get a part-time job, and maybe she would work, and somehow, with the help of the GI Bill of Rights, they would get by.

Darrell walked downtown to use a telephone. He called Coach Jim Tatum to tell him he would accept the standard scholarship offer and enroll at Oklahoma. Tatum, of course, was delighted.

On his way back to the room he and Edith had rented in Hollis, Darrell ran into a prosperous ex-student of OU who said he had been trying unsuccessfully to get in touch with him for several days.

"I just wanted to tell you," the enthusiastic alumnus declared, "that if you'll go to OU, I'll take care of your apartment rent, and your doctor bills, and make sure you and your family have enough to eat . . ."

Darrell, delighted, thanked him graciously and accepted his kind offer. Then he walked home, so happy that he stayed about ten feet above the ground, to tell Edith the good news. Tatum, meanwhile, was trying frantically to get Darrell's newly-discovered benefactor on the phone and tell him that Royal had agreed on the standard scholarship, so he did not need to offer any extra inducements.

By the time he made connections, he was probably about an hour late—and considerably more than a dollar short.

Chapter 5

PICKING UP AN OPTION

Darrell Royal still winces a little at the memory of how he rented a club coupe one day in January of 1946 and drove to Norman with his young wife and his baby daughter.

"We had everything we owned in that car," he recalls, "and there was still plenty of room left."

His possessions included that cast on his left arm—with spring football just around the corner. That compounded the traumatic experience, for the young veteran from Hollis, of enrolling at a school as large as the University of Oklahoma. But, somehow, he managed to get through registration—and even to dig deeply enough into his reservoir of courage to sign up for a course in public speaking.

"I had watched coaches enough to know that they had to be able to get up and talk," said Royal. "That's the only reason I registered for that course. And I really dreaded it. Our first assignment was to make a short speech—it wasn't supposed to be more than a minute or maybe a minute and a half long. But they assigned it about a month in advance. Well, there wasn't a day that went by during that month that I wasn't in sheer misery, just thinking about the day I'd have to get up in front of that class to give that talk. And it wasn't a big class, only about thirty people. But that was painful for me, really painful. I can't tell you how painful it was.

"It wasn't painful at all for me to talk in the locker room, visiting with other players. When I was in my own element, I was talking as much as anyone. But the thought of standing up and having everyone listen to me just gave me a real hangup.

"The teacher told us to talk about some experience we'd had, so I talked about visiting Birmingham, when I went through there on a trip to visit the Alabama campus. This was fresh on my mind, since Alabama was one of two or three schools I'd visited when I got out of the service and was trying to decide where to go to college.

"After all that suffering I did in advance, I managed to get up and give the speech without any trouble. But when I first went to the University of Oklahoma, I was really self-conscious. This was the first time I'd ever been around any kind of swank parties or country club atmosphere, where I was being introduced to people. It was a struggle for me just to shake hands and meet people, and stand there with any poise or confidence and talk to them. And I was twenty-one years old at the time.

"I remember the first time I was ever interviewed on the radio. It was by Hal Middlesworth, and it was just a very short thing—maybe twenty or thirty seconds. I was talking, but I wasn't conscious of what I was saying. I was just so excited and so ill at ease, talking into that microphone.

"Now I look back at that and ask myself why was it such a big deal, and why was I so nervous? I don't know—but I was."

On the football field, Royal didn't seem nervous at all; he ran, instead, as if he were just plain scared. And, to some extent, he *was* when the Sooners—with freshmen eligible—invaded West Point for their season-opener in 1946. Army, led by Doc "Mr. Inside" Blanchard and Glenn "Mr. Outside" Davis, was favored overwhelmingly in that game. The Cadets came from behind for a 21-7 victory which extended their winning streak to 19 games—but the versatile Royal attracted national attention while fighting a losing battle.

He also erased any doubt that his 159 pounds belonged in the starting lineup. He insists that he really was never aware of being small although he can look back now and see that his small stature really represented a handicap.

"I did try to put on weight, mainly because other people seemed to think it was so important," he said. "But I didn't like to weigh. I didn't like for other people to know what I weighed when they seemed to attach so much significance to weight."

Harold Keith, former sports information director at OU, recalls Royal as the back who could do more things "superbly" than any of the others developed during Bud Wilkinson's coaching regime there—but he also remembers him as the most sensitive player about his weight he ever saw.

"He would never get on the scales," said Keith, many years later. "He and I had a gentleman's agreement to list him in the program at a hundred and seventy pounds. I guess he was afraid the coaches wouldn't play him if they saw his real weight."

Royal tried everything from egg malts to beer, during his freshman year, in an effort to gain weight.

"Someone told me that if I'd drink a beer about an hour before my evening meal, it would settle my stomach and improve my appetite," he said. "I tried it for awhile but it didn't work. I ate 'way more than the average guy, anyway, but I still didn't put on weight. I was just a skinny kid and I wasn't going to be anything but a skinny kid."

A contributing factor in keeping his weight down undoubtedly was the amount of running he did, all year long. And after football practice each day, he usually kept burning up calories by staying on the field an extra hour or so to practice his punting. Frequently, a few youngsters

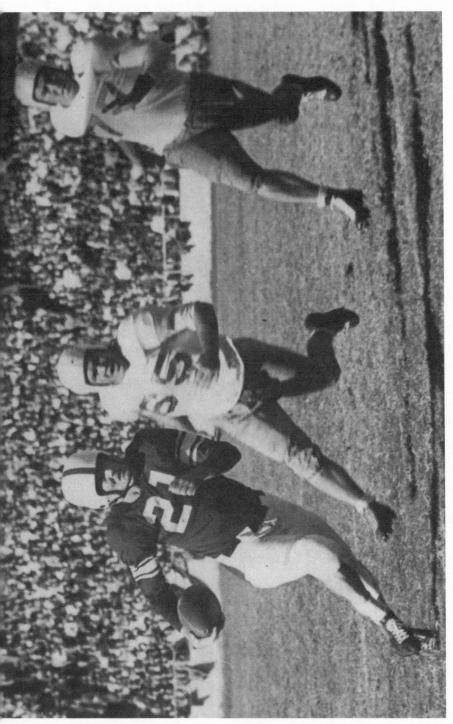

Royal makes a nice gain for Oklahoma in the 1946 Texas game as Spot Collins (65) and Harlan Wetz try to catch him. Texas won, 20-13.

would hang around to shag balls for him—and to listen to the tips he gave them on how to punt.

"That was part of getting 'em to stay—keeping 'em interested," Royal recalls. "One of the kids who used to hang around practice a lot up there was Gordon Roberts, whose father was on the OU faculty."

Roberts later followed Royal to Texas and played on his national championship team in 1963.

When he didn't have any shaggers to help, Royal usually would take a bagful of footballs and kick them—always picking out some target at which to aim—and then run down to the other end of the field to kick them all back. During the process, he usually managed to make contact with J. J. (Sarge) Dempsey, the Sooners' equipment manager.

"It would be almost dark and he'd come by and holler that he was leaving. He'd tell me to pull the door to when I left, to make sure I locked up.

"We ate at the training table across the street. I've gone over there many a night when the kitchen would be closed but they'd have a plate of food sitting out there for me. I'd usually holler earlier and ask 'em to leave something out for me. I didn't particularly care about the food being hot, and still don't. As a matter of fact, I don't like my food real hot."

Royal's punting and his expertise in holding the ball for Quarterback Dave Wallace's place kicks proved important factors in the Sooners' march to a 7-3 season during 1946, his freshman season. That record pleased just about everyone but Royal, who wanted to win 'em all. One of those losses was inflicted by the University of Texas, 20-13. Royal managed to net 46 yards in eight rushing attempts during that game and ran back four Texas kicks for a total of 92 yards; but he also had three of his six passes intercepted.

He was not at all pleased with his overall statistics for that season: a net of 126 yards on 58 rushing attempts, for an average of 2.1 yards per carry; 16 pass completions in 46 attempts, for a total of 207 yards and three touchdowns while getting seven intercepted.

But he did help the Sooners earn a bid to the first 'Gator Bowl Game—and then he almost got killed a short time before it was played. Driving to Hollis during the Christmas holidays, he went to sleep at the wheel and hit a concrete culvert.

Suddenly, his car sailed through the air like an airplane. It grazed the top of a large tree, shearing off the branches, and then turned upside down, landing in the bottom of a creek about 60 feet below the roadway. Somewhere during the midst of that dramatic flight, Royal was thrown from the car. He landed on the bank of the creek, with a scratch on his face which turned out to be the only visible souvenir of this terrifying experience.

His car was totally demolished.

"The wheels were still spinning," Royal said, "and I was sitting there on the bank—watching the anti-freeze from my car run down the creek, steaming—when this old farmer showed up. The first thing he wanted to know was if I'd hit his prize bull, which apparently had gotten outside his fence. He didn't ask if anyone else was in the car or anything else. He just wanted to know about his prize bull.

"I said, 'No, I didn't hit your bull—but if you've got a bucket, I'd like to catch some of that anti-freeze.'

"My thinking about the anti-freeze at that point was about as absurd as his thinking only about a bull, of course. It just shows what kind of thoughts go through your mind at a time like that. I thought at the time he was just worried about that bull. I guess he was worried mostly about the possibility that the bull might have caused the accident."

The farmer drove Royal into Duke, Oklahoma, about 20 miles from Hollis.

"I phoned my brother, Ray, to come get me and then I decided to lie down on the counter—we were in a little grocery store—to wait for him," said Royal. "By the time he got there, I was so stiff and sore I could hardly get up."

Notified by telephone of the accident, Coach Tatum insisted that Royal return to Norman for X-rays. The X-rays showed nothing had been broken.

"I couldn't even raise my arms, I was so stiff," Royal recalled. "I didn't work out at all before the 'Gator Bowl Game. But Coach Tatum told me a couple of days before the game to plan on making the trip. He said it might be the only bowl game I'd ever get to go to.

"We got down there and, just before the game, he suggested that I suit up. He said he thought I'd enjoy the game more if I suited up. And then, just before the kickoff, he said he'd probably start me if we kicked off—but he said I wouldn't have to tackle anybody, just play pass defense and punt.

"You know, it's a funny thing: I played most of the game and I felt better the next day than I had felt since the accident."

So did the Sooner fans, as they celebrated their 34-13 victory over North Carolina State.

A short while later, Tatum moved to the University of Maryland and Wilkinson was promoted from backfield coach to head coach at OU. Tatum and Wilkinson had installed the Split T formation at Oklahoma after picking it up at Iowa Preflight School, while coaching there with Don Faurot during World War II. As Wilkinson refined the formation, Royal soaked up everything he could learn about it in four years—and that had a tremendous impact on his career. It fact, he calls his own fabulously successful Wishbone T "just a souped-up version of the Split T."

As a crack defensive back, expert punter, offensive halfback and finally as a quarterback, Royal received about as complete a football education as any player could. But he still belittles his own ability as a player even though he made All-America in 1949, when he quarterbacked the Sooners to 11 consecutive victories.

"I really wasn't all that much of a football player," he declared. "I contributed and I could do *some* things. The one thing I could do that was exceptional, and I felt all along that I could do that all four years, was punt. But I worked like a dog on that. I could punt and play defense, and then, my senior year, I think I quarterbacked the team well. But my other three years, I made practically no contribution offensively.

"I wasn't much of a passer because my hand wasn't big enough. I had a good arm and could throw a rock or a baseball, something I could get a hold of, but I wasn't much of a passer. On the option, I used to like to suck them in on me so I could pitch out because that's where the big gainers were."

But Royal had all sorts of problems mastering the option play. During two-a-day practice sessions in September of 1949, after he had been demoted from the first team to the third, he got hit while running the option during a scrimmage—by a defensive end he didn't even see—and made a wild lateral.

"I went home and was sitting there and thinking about it, wondering what I could do to correct the problem," he recalled. "And the thought suddenly occurred to me that the only way I couldn't have seen the defensive end was by not looking at him. I just never really looked at him before, although I'd been told to. I couldn't wait to get to practice the next day. I started really looking at that defensive end and had no more problems with it."

Royal promptly told Wilkinson: Coach, you don't have to worry about that anymore, because I've got it, now; I know how to do it and I'm not ever going to have any trouble running the option again."

"Why?" asked Wilkinson.

"It's simple if you just keep your eye on the defensive end," Royal replied.

Wilkinson still delights in telling that story, putting perhaps a bit more emphasis than warranted on the number of times he had told Royal to do just that.

When he began coaching, Royal felt this was a point which could not be over-emphasized.

"I'd get over there and watch my quarterbacks to see if they were looking at the defensive end," he declared.

Royal attended summer school each year at OU (which enabled him to receive his business administration degree in January of 1950) and worked part-time during the summers, usually as a laborer on construction work. But there were exceptions to that work pattern—and one of the most exceptional was his stint as a life guard, despite the fact that he couldn't even swim across the pool and back.

"They had me guard the shallow end, where the little kids were," he explained.

During the football season, he also found ample opportunity to try out the free enterprise system.

"Ozzie Marr ran a drug store in Norman," he said. "Newt Trotter and I used to borrow money from him to buy Texas-Oklahoma football tickets. We'd buy as many as we could when they first went on sale, and then we could always get at least ten or fifteen dollars apiece for them just before the game. I'd sometimes sell maybe twenty or thirty tickets, and that was a heckuva lot of money in those days. But it wasn't any put-up job. Nobody made a deal with us; we were just looking ahead, knowing the game always was a sell-out."

No matter what else he was doing, Royal found time to work out almost every day of the year and that was an investment of time which paid rich dividends, especially in the punting department.

One of the most dramatic demonstrations of that came during 1947, his sophomore season, against the heavily-favored Missouri Tigers. Royal punted out of bounds on the one-, four- and three-yard lines during that game. The latter punt came during the fourth quarter, with Missouri holding a 12-7 lead, and led to a fumble on the next play. The Sooners quickly scored their second touchdown and went on to pull one of college football's biggest upsets that day, 21-12.

Royal had to sit out the 1947 Texas game with an injury but one of his biggest college thrills came in 1948, when he played a key role in Oklahoma's first victory over the Longhorns since 1939. He set up the Sooners' first touchdown with a 10-yard run to the 2, completed two passes in three attempts, three times prevented what appeared to be sure Texas touchdowns and did his usual masterful punting job. The final score was Oklahoma 20, Texas 14—and Royal quarterbacked the Sooners to a duplicate of that victory in 1949, 20-14. He rushed for 34 yards that day, punted seven times for a 45-yard average, did a superb job calling plays, passed for one touchdown and threw a goal-line block that permitted George Thomas to score on a 20-yard run.

The Sooners went to the Sugar Bowl after both the 1948 and 1949 seasons. They upset North Carolina (led by the great Charley "Choo Choo" Justice), 14-6, on Jan. 1, 1949, and clobbered LSU, 35-0, a year later. Royal, only five feet 10 inches tall, drew many superlatives for shackling North Carolina's great pass receiver, Art Weiner, who was six inches taller, and also for his punting, passing and running.

The University of Oklahoma record book, still sprinkled liberally with Royal's name, notes among "exceptional performances" in punting: "In the 1949 and 1950 Sugar Bowl games, Darrell Royal punted a total of 15 times, angling 13 over either the North Carolina and Louisiana State sideline or end-line. Only two punts stayed in the field of play."

The same book notes that Royal set OU records for the longest punt return (95 yards against Kansas, 1948), most passes intercepted in three seasons (15) and in four seasons (17), and the longest punt (81 yards against Oklahoma A&M, 1948).

During the 1948 season, he also returned eight punts for 263 yards and a 32.8-yard average, the school's highest in history at that time.

And the young man who later was to acquire a not-very-accurate reputation for disdaining the forward pass threw 76 consecutive passes without an interception during the 1948 and 1949 seasons before an Oklahoma Aggie halfback picked one off.

During those two seasons, Royal completed 54 percent of his passes—hitting 54 in 100 attempts for a total of 811 yards and nine touchdowns.

But the statistics don't come close to describing Royal's playing career at Oklahoma. A more accurate evaluation of his achievements appeared on Jan. 4, 1950, after his final game against LSU in the Sugar Bowl, in a column written by Walter Stewart for the *Memphis Commercial-Appeal*:

Darrell Royal, Oklahoma quarterback, owns one of the most brilliant masses of football cerebellum we've seen caged in one skull. As the skilled duelist probes for weakness in the blade of his antagonist, Darrell spent the first period deep in technical research. But once he'd solved the pattern, he launched his form and drove it downfield with a gathered fury which matched that of Stonewall Jackson. We've never witnessed better play selection, and that night he gave us a clinical critique which was magnificently lucid and economically complete. He'll make someone a game-winning coach . . . .

Chapter 6

SCOUTING AROUND

Royal's phenomenal coaching career started on a strange, incongruous note which might be described as "prudent impatience." He failed to get an assistant's job he wanted, at Vanderbilt, while refusing to be interviewed for the *head coaching job* at Abilene Christian College.

As a man with a family when he was graduated from Oklahoma, he knew he could not afford the luxury of waiting around for the "right" opportunity. But he desperately wanted to get into college coaching.

So when Coach Bill Edwards of Vanderbilt invited him to Nashville for an interview, he jumped at the chance. That turned out to be the only job he ever was interviewed for which was not offered to him. And, although he was sorely disappointed at the time, he looks back at that incident now with the feeling that it may have a blessing in disguise.

"Vanderbilt was going to run the Straight T formation, which I'd had no experience at all with," said Royal. "I wasn't too sure of my footing. I felt like I could learn it but I could see why Bill Edwards didn't want to hire me."

Royal's later conversion from the Church of Christ to Presbyterianism, and predestination, may have done much to convince him that it all worked out for the best.

He had an offer to become head coach at El Reno High School, about 50 miles from Norman. And if his ego was wounded, as it was, by the failure of Vanderbilt to hire him, it was healed almost immediately by the approach from Abilene Christian.

The legendary Tonto Coleman, a fellow Church of Christ member who had become a friend of Royal's during their service football days, decided to leave ACC for a coaching job at the University of Florida. He recommended that ACC interview Royal as a possible successor.

The president of ACC called Royal and said he would like to interview him about "a coaching job."

"What kind of coaching job?" asked Royal.

"The head coaching job," he was told.

"The *head* job?"

"Yes, we're interested in talking to you about becoming head coach at ACC."

A moment of stunned silence followed.

"Well," said Royal, "I've been offered a high school job and I really believe I'd better take that . . . ."

Looking back, Royal shakes his head and declares: "That really sounds kinda screwy for me to take the El Reno High School job and not even go talk to ACC about the head coaching job, but I just didn't think I was ready. I've had confidence in every job I've accepted but I didn't have any confidence then about stepping in and becoming the head coach at a four-year college. To this day, I don't think I was qualified. And there's no telling what would have happened to me if I'd gone out there and they'd hired me.

"I needed a little experience to get my feet on the ground," he added.

What he really wanted was an assistant coaching job on a college staff. So when he signed a contract with El Reno on Feb. 6, it was with the understanding that if he received a college coaching offer by June, he could take it; otherwise, he would coach El Reno High School at least for the 1950 season.

He began commuting from Norman to El Reno, teaching "study hall" and a class in the "Theory of Football" at El Reno High.

"I remember what a shock it was to me," said Royal, "when I got into the real details of football and realized how much I didn't know. But at least I was smart enough to know that I didn't know, and to back away until I could get back and check with somebody who did."

He began spending much of his spare time at the University of Oklahoma's spring practice sessions, where the Split T still was in full bloom. Coach Beattie Feathers of North Carolina State and his athletics director, Roy Clogston, visited Norman to take a close look at this remarkable formation—and decided they wanted someone to help them install it at NCS. Wilkinson recommended Royal.

On March 14, 1950, Royal made the first of seven job changes which, during the next eight years, would take him to the Valhalla he found at the University of Texas.

Royal hustled over to Raleigh, North Carolina, in time for spring training—and also in time to play an instrumental role in getting Feathers to hire Wade Walker, with whom he had played at Oklahoma, as line coach.

Everything seemed to be coming up roses—until Royal had to make his first speech to a high school football banquet.

"I got up to talk," he recalled, years later, "and drew a complete blank. If you've never had this happen to you, you don't know how frightful it is and how painful it is. But I got up and just flat couldn't talk; I couldn't say a thing. I finally just said, 'I'm sorry,' and sat down.

"Of course, I was so embarrassed that all I wanted was out of there. But I had to sit there, and I didn't want to look out at the people attending the banquet. I felt like they were all looking at me, and they probably were. But they were really feeling sorry for me, I imagine, looking back on it. But I was really miserable and I couldn't wait 'til that thing was over. Seemed like it lasted a lifetime.

"They gave me a set of cuff links for coming there to be their speaker. When I finally got outside and back to my car, I looked at those cuff links, then hauled off and threw 'em just as far as I could throw 'em. I've often wondered if somebody found 'em later and wondered what had happened.

"So then, I'm driving out of there, and I've got another banquet the next night in Durham. And that was a long ol' ride. Now, I've got to decide if I'm going to stay in coaching, and try to whip this thing, or get out and try to do something else. I just kept thinking about what would happen if I got up and drew a blank again."

After several hours of self-searching agony, he reached the conclusion that there was no way he could get out of coaching. He would just have to master the art of public speaking, he decided.

"I made up my mind that I would keep my speech in Durham so simple that I couldn't draw a blank there," he said. "I'd just have a few sentences to say, which I did."

He managed to get through the Durham speech without any trouble but the public speaking problem was destined to plague him for years—even until after he became firmly entrenched at Texas.

"I still have a hangup as far as reading anything is concerned," Royal said after winning his third national championship. "If I have to read a radio or TV commercial, for instance, I have a hangup. I can't even read 'Mary Had a Little Lamb.' I blow it. Just the simplest of words. But if you give me a thought and let me express it in my own words, I can do that without any trouble.

"I no longer have any hangup at all about talking to the press, or to a crowd. It doesn't matter now whether it's five or five thousand people I'm talking to. This is something that I know can be licked, *because I had to do it!"*

In late July of 1950, Royal lectured on the Split T formation at a University of Tennessee coaching clinic. His presentation lasted one hour, to the second. And it made a tremendous impression on some of the most successful coaches in the business.

"I was really in awe of many of the people who were there—such as Coaches Bob Neyland, Herman Hickman and Beattie Feathers," said Royal. "But I didn't have any problem because I knew my subject and I was in my element. Of course, I really worked on that presentation in advance. I timed it to the second. I mean I knew exactly what point I was supposed to be making every *second*, not just every *minute*, during that hour.

"That speech really helped me, partly because General Neyland was there and he had some very nice things to say about it, such as how surprised he was to find I was that knowledgeable about the Split T, as a player. This was when the Split T was still fairly new and a bunch of coaches were looking for people who knew something about it. I had that thing more organized than any lecture I've ever given, anywhere."

As impressive as it was, the lecture probably did not gain Royal any more prestige than did the scouting job he performed that fall on the University of Maryland. North Carolina State upset the eighth-ranked Terps, 16-13; Maryland Coach Tatum, who had coached Royal during his freshman year at OU, gave much of the credit to his erstwhile charge.

"There's no question about Darrell Royal's scouting being a big factor," Tatum said after the game. "Royal played quarterback in the Split T at Oklahoma last year and he learned everything that worries a Split T quarterback. He was able to tell the State players how to worry our Jack Scarbath.

"That's why we lost the ball early in the game, and losing the ball got us behind. I didn't figure Royal close enough, because he worked out the one defect in our offense—and that was that Scarbath was short on experience."

Royal did figure that the same things which bothered him, when he was a Split T quarterback short on experience, would bother Scarbath.

"I watched some film on Scarbath," Royal recalled, "and saw that he went through a definite ritual before he'd pitch back. People had been waiting, every game, and he'd go out there and dance around. I never had seen anybody go in there and get him before he went into that routine. And I remembered that I hadn't learned until my senior year how to react to those people who really jumped in there on you.

"I could handle those people who sagged back there and waited. I didn't figure Scarbath would have much trouble with that kind but I didn't know how much training he'd had on the kind that crash on in. And I knew that if a quarterback hadn't really been trained on somebody jumping up in his face, and jumping in it in a hurry, it might cause some bad laterals.

"And, what the heck, we were big underdogs. So I recommended to Coach Feathers, and he went along with it, that we have our end jump in—shoot in, instead of sagging back. Not all the time, but most of the time. Then we'd revolve the halfback up fast and bring the safety over quick, to cover.

"We did get some bad pitches and I did have some input on the thing. But some of the credit I received was just a case of my former coach throwing a fish to one of his former players."

Regardless of how much they may or may not have been deserved, Tatum's remarks gave an added boost to Royal's meteoric career. And by the end of the 1950 season, Coach Buddy Brothers wanted to add Royal to his staff at the University of Tulsa, as backfield coach.

Royal flew to Tulsa for an interview. Within a few hours, he was offered an assistant's job, at what he remembers as "a pretty good raise in pay," and accepted it. Then he went to the home of a good friend, H. B. Dowell (with whose son, Charley, he had played football at Oklahoma) to spend the night. Dowell informed him that Bud Wilkinson had been trying to get in touch with him.

Royal returned Wilkinson's call and received one of the most pleasant surprises of his young life.

"We have an opening on the staff," said Wilkinson. "We'd like very much to have you join us."

Royal, somewhat stunned, told his old coach what had just transpired in Tulsa.

"Let me talk to Coach Brothers," he said, "and I'll call you back."

Royal called Brothers and told him about Wilkinson's call, making it clear that he would like to return to his alma mater.

"We offered you a job and you took it," Brothers said, rather coldly. "I assumed it was all firm."

"That's right," said Royal, who had not yet signed a contract with Tulsa. "And if you aren't willing for me to go to Oklahoma, and with good feelings, forget it—and this is the last time it will ever be mentioned. I'll be here and I'll be happy, because I appreciate the offer of the job at Tulsa."

"Well," said Brothers, "I think you ought to stay by your commitment."

"Fine," said Royal. "I will."

He then called Wilkinson and explained the situation, regretfully turning down the OU job.

"But, as it turned out," Royal said, many years later, "it probably was the best thing for me because things have broken so well for me in the coaching profession since that time. And I don't know what would have happened if I had gone to Oklahoma. Sometimes, it's better to branch out and get under other people and learn other ideas and other methods and other thinking, than to stay under one guy all the time . . . ."

The 1951 season, at Tulsa, turned out to be what Royal considers one of the most productive of his internship "because Coach Brothers really gave me a free hand with the offensive backs, and even with directing the offense during games."

"I talked to the quarterbacks directly during our games, instructing them on what to call," said Royal. "I worked from a pressbox behind the goal posts at one end of the field and I still feel that is probably the best way to look at a game, from the standpoint of picking up the other team's defenses. You're looking right down the back of 'em. You can tell whether they're on the shoulder shade, or heads up, or whether they've got a stunt on. It's really easy to tell.

"I'd get a couple of high school coaches to sit beside me and I'd give them specific segments of the defense to watch; then I watched certain segments of it, so we could pick up their defensive patterns pretty fast.

Then I'd talk to the quarterbacks on the sideline telephone and tell them what we wanted to concentrate on during the next series.

"Coach Brothers' giving me all the authority and freedom, and the fact that he expressed that much confidence in me, made me work that much harder. So it was an excellent year for me as far as learning about coaching and instructing the Split T."

Murray Warmath, at Mississippi State, dutifully noted the results (a 9-1 season) and offered Royal a job as his assistant.

"It was a little more money, but not enough to warrant the move," Royal recalls. "But Tulsa was in the Missouri Valley Conference and Mississippi State, although not a power, was in the Southeastern Conference. I was moving up to a more recognized conference, really, and that was the main reason I took the job. At Mississippi State, we were playing people like Tennessee and Kentucky and LSU and Alabama, instead of Wichita, Cincinnati, Marquette . . . ."

Warmath also gave Royal a lot of freedom in handling the offense, which combined the Split T with the Army series which Warmath had learned under Red Blaik at West Point.

"Coach Warmath talked directly to the quarterbacks and I talked directly to him, on the telephone from the pressbox—which is pretty much the system we use here at Texas," said Royal. "I didn't talk directly to the quarterbacks but many times he'd use my suggestions. And he'd also call things on his own."

Meanwhile, Royal's reputation as a specialist on the splendid Split T was spreading—even beyond the borders of the United States. One of his old Oklahoma teammates, Claude Arnold, was playing professional football for the Edmonton Eskimos in Canada when a coaching vacancy developed there. Arnold suggested that the Eskimos interview Royal. They did, and he quickly took his first head coaching job—although he had never seen a professional football game, in the United States or Canada.

But the Eskimos offered him $13,500 a year; at that time, it sounded to Royal like all the money in the world.

Chapter 7

IN TRANSIT

Like a great many other wives, Edith Royal has compiled scrapbooks containing newspaper clippings, telegrams, letters and photographs pertaining to her husband's career. Pasted on the inside front cover of one spanning the years 1953 through 1956 is a picture clipped from an old *Saturday Evening Post*, which seems most appropriate: it shows a moving van and a well-loaded family car preparing to leave a just-vacated house, as five neighborhood youngsters sadly wave good-by.

That scrapbook's first entry is a clipping from the Feb. 16, 1953, *Edmonton* (Canada) *Journal*. It described a weekend visit by Royal to confer with officials of the Edmonton Eskimos about their head coaching job. The article noted that, although Royal was only 28 years old, he was "a very personable young man" who "caused a favorable reaction among the Edmonton football moguls" and that he "lacks nothing in the way of qualifications."

An article from the *Winnipeg Free Press* two days later said Royal had resigned as an assistant coach at Mississippi State to sign a three-year contract as head coach of the Edmonton team in the Western Interprovincial Football Union.

"There was a lot of doubt in the minds of many people about whether I could handle that job," Royal recalls. "I had confidence I could handle it or I never would have taken it.

"They asked me right off the bat what formation I was going to use and I said the Split T. There were a lot of guys coaching up there that kinda put down the idea that you could run the Split T in professional football—up in that league, anyway. As it turned out, we had a very successful year and gained more yardage than any other team in Canada.

"But it was the hardest year I've ever gone through, in some ways, mainly because I was faced for the first time with cutting guys off from their livelihood—guys who had worked hard, were dedicated and had put everything into the program that they possibly could. Most of 'em were just about my age. And in some cases, it was just tissue-paper thin as to whether you'd keep this one or that one. But you had to let one or the other go. That's one of the hardest things I ever had to do, and I lost about fifteen pounds that season."

While Royal was losing weight, he was winning most of his games. The Eskimos fashioned a 17-5 record and won their division easily—with another University of Oklahoma product, Halfback Billy Vessels, leading the way. But they lost a heart-breaking, decisive playoff game during the last two minutes when a flat pass from Royal's old buddy, Arnold, ricocheted off the intended receiver and bounced into the hands of a Winnipeg defender, who took it back all the way for the winning touchdown.

"Claude threw that pass well," Royal recalls as he dredges up that painful memory. "It was right on target but it hit the receiver and bounced off. But the worst part was that we were down on Winnipeg's fifteen yard-line, with the score tied, when we tried it. We could have had a cinch rouge that would have won the game."

A "rouge" is a one-point play, popular in Canadian football, which Royal still would like to see adopted in the United States. Any time you kick the ball over the opponents' goal line and they fail to run it out, you get one point. End zones 20 yards deep (the playing field itself is 120 yards long) help make this feasible, according to Royal.

"We've got an unfair rule in our game," he declared. "The receiving team catches a punt in the end zone and we give 'em twenty yards for nothing. There's nothing fair about that. Why should a team be given twenty yards because you got it too close to their goal line before you kicked?

"That's like paying people not to grow hogs or not to grow cotton. I never have understood that, any more than I understand why it is that if you punt the ball out of your own end zone and it goes sixty yards, you get all sixty—but if you get to the other team's forty and then kick it sixty, they penalize you twenty yards.

"They oughta give you a rouge. That'd make 'em run it out of the end zone and the fans would get more for their money. In Canada, you don't see people catching that ball in the end zone and then staying there, unless they want to give up a point."

Despite the differences in rules and field dimensions, Royal had no trouble adjusting to Canadian pro football.

"It's still basic fundamentals that win up there just like anywhere else: blocking, tackling, throwing, catching, running," he remarked.

"And that pass interception that cost us the playoff game merely drove home something I already believed in," he said. "It made me more conservative, I guess, if you want to call it being conservative."

Royal still was being hailed as a sort of king of the Klondike on Feb. 1, 1954, when the story broke that he was resigning to become head coach at Mississippi State. Warmath had accepted the head coaching job at the University of Minnesota and Mississippi State was giving Royal a four-year contract at $15,000 a year to replace him.

There was the matter of two more years remaining on Royal's

Edmonton contract and, at first, that caused a bit of static.

"I went to see our Board of Directors and told them I'd like to take the Mississippi State job," said Royal. "I told them I'd always wanted to be a head coach at a major American college and the only reason I'd been willing to sign a three-year contract up there was that I thought it would take me at least three years to get an opportunity. But the opportunity just came along sooner than I had anticipated.

"At first, they sorta balked. They said, 'Well, you've got a contract here and we think you ought to stick by it.' I got to looking at that contract and found they could buy me off for sixty-five hundred dollars, total, any day they wanted to. So that kind of contract wasn't protecting me very much. I finally reasoned with them and convinced them that coaching in college really was my ambition, so they turned me loose. But I didn't know much about contracts, at that point. I did get a thousand dollar bonus up there for winning our division and I would have gotten another thousand if we'd won that playoff game."

Royal insists that none of his moves were made for higher pay but strictly for advancement within the profession. As a matter of fact, he added, he would have been in bad financial straits had the schools which hired him not paid his moving expenses.

"Someone said that three moves is equal to a fire, and they're right," he declared. "It's just like being burned out when you've moved three times, it's so expensive."

For the most part, Royal managed his moves so tactfully that employers left holding unfulfilled contracts really didn't seem to mind. When he left Edmonton, for instance, he was quoted as saying his appointment to the Mississippi State job would make "a lot of good young coaches forget the feeling that you are buried if you come up here—it should kill the idea that if you come to Canada to coach you cut yourself off from football affairs in the States and become a homeless exile."

Jim Brooke, writing a sports column for the *Edmonton Journal*, agreed with that idea. He went on to say:

"Although a minority here may regard Royal as a turncoat in a class with Benedict Arnold and Lord Haw Haw, your agent's reaction has been one of mirthful amazement and admiration.

"Here is a young man who has actually beaten the racket. He walked through the deadly minefield of one WIFU season, suffering only superficial wounds while his coaching contemporaries were being mown down like the Boche at Bastogne. And then he calmly quit while he was ahead of the (Canadian) game. No other coach can make that statement.

"The mortality rate in Western Canada football coaching circles is so high that Lloyds of London would go broke in a week if they started to lay the odds. More power to the survivor.

"And the beauty of it is that Royal has yet to apply for his first coaching job. Some people are lucky—and others are like Darrell K. Royal.

"This boy makes the original personality kid look like a deaf mute in a dungeon. His ability to leave his bosses laughing should serve as a criterion for every bigtime comedian from Bob Hope right on down to (Uggg!) Jerry Lewis.

"Although he didn't aggressively seek any new position for the 1954 football seminar, Royal was actually approached by three (count 'em) colleges in one sense or another. And all three schools had employed him at various stages in his career.

"Royal had a nibble from North Carolina State, where the head coach's post has since been filled; he was told by Tulsa University people that he was included in their future football plans; and he was hired by Mississippi State," Brooke noted.

In a news article announcing Royal's departure, Brooke commented:

"Technically speaking, Royal was probably the best coach the western conference has seen to date. The former Oklahoma All-America quarterback drilled his club in the fundamentals and despite his youth commanded the full respect and attention of his players.

"Royal's technique of using films of games to correct mistakes and check players was a revelation to Western Canada football insiders who were used to the slipshod, hit-or-miss approach of the old pros.

"The young coach, by reason of his pleasant personality and ability to think on his feet, was extremely popular with the Edmonton fans and his lectures and film commentaries regularly packed Touchdown Club meetings and other functions . . . ."

Royal needed all the assets he could muster in his new job.

Mississippi State's prospects looked bleak when Royal took over—especially since Jackie Parker, a brilliant back whom Royal had helped develop there in 1952, had graduated. Still, Royal regarded his opportunity as a great one.

"I don't believe anyone who gets his first head coaching job is going to find a warm bed made for him, unless he is extremely lucky," he remarked philosophically. "About the only time that happens is when a man has been on a staff for some time, and the staff has been successful, a good program has been built up, and the head coach resigns. And in a case like that, it's usually an older man who gets the job."

But by the middle of the 1954 season, more and more people were beginning to discuss the remarkable similarities in the coaching styles of Royal and his old tutor, Bud Wilkinson. When Royal's Mississippi State Maroons visited Miami for a game with the University of Miami, Norris Anderson wrote in the *Miami Daily News*:

"Wilkinson and his pupil, Royal, both resemble young men whose greatest worries never happened.

"Basically, they are uncomplicated, affable souls. Yet, chat with either before a game and their words are fringed in darkest crepe and bereft of any semblance of hope. If it's the credo of the profession, Wilkinson and Royal own the basic copyrights.

"Mental telepathy between the pair is restricted to 'a phone call once in a while,' yet Royal will be first to admit that his entire offense is patterned off Poppa Bud's Split T.

"'We don't look much like Oklahoma, but we try to,' Royal commented...."

They didn't look much like Oklahoma at all in losing to Miami, 27-13. That left the Maroons with a 3-2 won-lost record going into their clash the following week with their old nemesis, Alabama, which they had not beaten since 1941.

Alabama was favored by 18 points in its homecoming game with Mississippi State at Tuscaloosa. But the Crimson Tide was unable to score until 25 seconds before halftime, when it converted a fumble recovery at the State 37 into a touchdown and took a 7-0 lead.

Early in the third quarter, State Halfback Bobby Collins took a Tide punt, faked a handoff and raced 59 yards for a touchdown. But the extra point try was blocked, leaving Alabama ahead, 7-6.

Finally, with nine minutes left to play, the Maroons recovered a fumble on the Tide 30 and then Halfback Joe Silveri raced 30 yards around end for a 12-7 victory—one that was called the biggest upset win in Mississippi State history.

Royal, who was carried off the field on the shoulders of his jubilant players, still recalls it as one of the highlights of his coaching career.

But then, suffering from an epidemic of injuries, his Maroons lost their last three games. That left him with the first of what turned out to be two consecutive 6-4 seasons at Mississippi State.

While the record alone was not enough to attract national attention, University of Washington Athletics Director George Briggs picked up many glowing recommendations of Royal from the coaches' grapevine as he searched for a new football coach. Washington had just fired John Cherberg, primarily because of a scandal involving alleged payoffs to football players rather than because of his 5-4-1 record in 1955.

Briggs phoned Royal and asked him to meet him in a Memphis hotel to discuss the job. It did not take long for Briggs to hire Royal on a four-year contract at $17,000 a year.

"I'd never been in the State of Washington before," Royal recalls. "The day I drove into Seattle to take over that job was the first time I'd ever been there. But I knew it was a state university, I knew what their enrollment was, what their budget was, what their attendance was at football games, what kind of stadium they had, what the population was, and how many high schools were playing football in the State of Washington.

"You don't really have to visit a campus, if you know these things, to decide if you want to work there. You can look over their won-lost records for the past twenty years and tell a lot about them. I wouldn't have to visit Michigan, for instance, to know that that's an outstanding coaching job—or Southern Cal, or LSU, or Oklahoma, or Alabama . . . .

"The main reason I left Mississippi State for Washington was that Washington was a school that had enjoyed more success. Mississippi State had never won a conference championship and they'd been in a bowl game only one time, the Orange Bowl. And it was very hard to recruit against Ole Miss. I felt, and still feel, there are some natural advantages to being at state universities. I decided *that* after coaching at North Carolina State, Mississippi State, and the University of Tulsa—and competing against state universities. I was going to a state university at Washington."

He did not even suspect, however, what a furor his hiring would provoke—simply because he was to be paid the then-fabulous salary of $17,000 a year.

The controversy began when the campus newspaper, the *Washington Daily*, polled the school's faculty on the matter. It reported that 79 percent of the faculty felt football should be de-emphasized and 81 percent thought the new coach's salary was too high.

Time magazine promptly picked up the cudgel and declared that "the facultymen had reason for outrage" since the average pay for a full professor outside the professional schools was $8,469.

Sports Columnist Emmett Watson noted a few days later, however, in the *Seattle Post-Intelligencer*, that football coaches usually get paid more than professors because they get fired more often than professors—and any job with a high turnover usually commands good money. He quoted an unidentified coach as saying: "A biology professor can flunk 25 percent of his class and nobody pays any attention. But let Royal send a football team out next fall that flunks one test in front of 50,000 people, and he's in thick soup."

Watson added:

"The conclusion is clear: big-time football is a thing apart from university education, and a professor might as well fret over the salary paid Groucho Marx as worry about how much the football coach makes.

"Both are in the entertainment business, and both had better produce—or else.

"As a sort of a flat footnote to this whole rhubarb, I conducted my own poll among football coaches. 'Is Royal's salary too high?' they were asked.

"A funny coincidence occurs here: 81 percent said 'Hell, no!'"

A few days later, Melvin Durslag sized up Royal in his *Los Angeles Herald-Examiner* sports column as "the prototype of the young man in big-time college coaching today."

"He was clean cut, attired trimly in a good suit to which the sox matched," Durslag wrote of Royal's appearance at a cocktail party. "The knot in his tie was neat and he spoke firmly, yet modestly, guarding his statements carefully in matters that might have required guarding.

"He was like a lieutenant recently out of Officers Candidate School who knew his manual well and was not going to foul up in his biggest command to date.

"The modern young football coach is no longer the lovable slob, or the cracker barrel con artist, or the phony moralist of the old days. He is a cool, sharpshooting business executive who, without stepping out of character, might sell oil stocks just as easily . . . ."

Durslag concluded that column with the observation: "Well, for the most part, Royal seems like a decent enough fellow. Let's not hang him at least until he loses his opener."

Royal recognized the fact that a few people were anxious to hang him right then—and just because he had come there from Mississippi. In their zeal to eliminate racial discrimination, they were inclined to discriminate against him simply because he was a Southerner. They noted that the Washington team included several Negroes and they asked how a coach from Mississippi could be expected to work with them.

To Royal, this seemed the least of his problems. He and Edith had become close friends, while in Canada, with Rollie Miles, the first black to play for him, and Miles' wife.

"I guess they were the first real close black friends I had," Royal recalled, "and the first ones I really became concerned about. That was in 1953. But our black maid in Mississippi apparently didn't feel she'd been too mistreated or she wouldn't have named her son 'Darrell Royal Reese'."

Royal figured correctly that a few victories would take care of both the salary criticism and the senseless speculation about possible racial problems. Shortly after taking the Washington job, he told a sportswriter he understood the situation there perfectly.

"In visits with alumni in Los Angeles, San Francisco and Seattle," he said, "I've found that they're all behind us—win or tie!"

Ironically, the totally unfounded, speculative slurs about his relationship with blacks were the first in a series of incidents destined to haunt him for years, giving him a false image in the eyes of many.

But shortly after that 1956 season opened, Royal Brougham wrote in his *Seattle Post-Intelligencer* sports column:

"Integration—Almost unnoticed is the way head coach Royal has handled what might have been a grave problem. When it was learned that Washington was importing a head coach and several assistants from the Deep South, there was much eyebrow-lifting among the skeptics who noted the presence of a half-dozen Negro stars on the squad. Mississippi? That's a lynchin' country. That's where they have changed the

Constitution to read—'Liberty, Equality and Justice for all, unless your skin is dark.'

"Firmly, skillfully and quietly, the coaches licked the problem. No favorites, no discrimination, a fair deal for all. Results: Credell Green, Luther Carr, Bobby Herring and Jim Jones are the scoring punch in the UW backfield. And Coach Royal has complete harmony in the ranks. Moral: Teaching men to block, tackle and run with the ball is only a part of a football coach's job."

Royal compiled a 5-5 record during that 1956 season and tied for fourth in the tough Pacific Coast Conference. That was considered quite remarkable, especially since the Huskies suffered four straight losses while their two top quarterbacks were sidelined with injuries. They also sent shock waves all along the coast by upsetting Stanford, 34-13, before polishing off Washington State, 40-26, in their season finale.

During the latter part of the season, Royal had kept an attentive ear tuned in—via Atlanta, Georgia, of all places—on the University of Texas' search for a new football coach. Ed Price, in the midst of a disastrous 1-9 season, had announced on October 31 that he would resign at the end of the year.

"I've always been a dreamer, even as a little kid," said Royal, "and I've always daydreamed in positive ways—about kicking a ball 90 yards, or running faster than I could ever run, or getting coaching jobs that I could never really have a chance to get. And I'd always daydreamed about coaching at the University of Texas.

"No, I never did any daydreaming about coaching at the University of Oklahoma. The only one I ever daydreamed about was the University of Texas. I don't know what caused that, except we lived just five miles from the border of Texas and we always competed against Texas schools, without much success...."

His chances of getting the Texas job, even a week before he was hired, seemed almost nil; at that point, the Longhorns' list of prospects included 100 names and "Royal" was not one of them.

But Tonto Coleman, then a member of Bobby Dodd's staff at Georgia Tech, stayed in contact with him about it and told him not to give up. Since Dodd was one of the top prospects, and then served as something of an adviser to Texas after turning down the job, Coleman knew up to the minute what was going on in Austin. And he repeatedly reminded Dodd that Royal appeared to be one of the brightest of the young coaches.

At the same time, Coleman periodically advised Royal: "It looks pretty remote but I wouldn't give up. You know, the Lord works in mysterious ways. I just don't think the odds are very good."

Coleman later recalled that Royal first attracted his attention while playing for the Third Air Force. Coleman was a scout for the Fort Worth Skymasters—and those introductions of "Darrell Royal, Hollis High

School" sandwiched between the names of former All-Americans made him curious enough to want to get acquainted.

The two quickly became good friends.

"And Tonto," Royal remarked, "is full of affection for his friends. I don't guess there's anybody that cares and thinks and worries more about his friends than Tonto does.

"He was the only living person I was talking to about the Texas job, and I knew my name wasn't even on the list. But finally, he called one day and said, 'Well, I got your name in the hat.' Of course, that was all he could do but that was a lot, and I really appreciated it."

Dana X. Bible, the former Texas coach who led a Longhorn renaissance (from 1937 through 1946), was about to retire as Director of Athletics and he spearheaded the search for a new coach. He compiled two lists—one of men who could be expected to serve in the dual capacity of head football coach and athletics director and the other of coaches only.

Dodd and Duffy Daugherty of Michigan State topped the first list. Bible recalls that when they indicated they were not interested in moving to Texas, both gave enthusiastic recommendations of Royal as one of the best young coaches in the business.

About the same time, Athletics Director Matty Bell of SMU contacted Royal about the head coaching job there. When Bell asked Royal if he were interested in it, the young Washington coach said he was—primarily because he was anxious to move back to the Southwest. But Royal much preferred coaching at a state university over the same job at a church school, so he exercised great restraint. Bell told him he probably would call him back.

"I was sweating out the Texas thing at the time," Royal recalled. "I didn't want to slam the door on SMU since I really had no reason to hang on for Texas. But I didn't want to get involved with SMU because I just kinda felt like something might happen at Texas. And, finally, I got that call; I never will forget that."

It came one December night after the Royals had gone to bed. Darrell answered the phone and the operator said, "Long distance calling Mr. Darrell Royal."

"This is he."

Then came the deep, booming voice of Bible.

"Coach Royal, this is D.X. Bible of the University of Texas."

Royal's face lighted up so much he really did not need to tell his wife who was calling, but he put his hand over the mouthpiece of the phone and said, "This is it, Edith—it's the University of Texas!"

Darrell Royal loved coaching during games, even after the lustre of his off-field duties began to dim. He was a superb field general.

Chapter 8

THAT GREENER GRASS

"I told Mr. Bible I'd be delighted to come to Austin for an interview—and then I didn't sleep the rest of the night," said Royal. "The next morning, I called him back, just as early as I dared, to ask him who would be interviewing me, so I could kinda get their rank and smell."

Bible gave him a brief rundown on the Athletic Council and the Board of Regents. He also suggested that Royal travel under an assumed name, in order to avoid speculation.

Royal promptly told Briggs, still the Director of Athletics at Washington, about the trip and indicated that he planned to take the job if it were offered.

Royal decided to travel under the name of Jim Pittman, one of his top assistants. Pittman didn't mind that at all, especially since he and his wife were tired of the long rainy season in Seattle and were anxious to move closer to home. And he had no doubt that Royal would get the job. In fact, Pittman and Mike Campbell, Royal's other top assistant, had so much confidence in their boss that they told their wives, as soon as they found out he was going to Austin for an interview, to stop buying groceries and start packing.

When Royal stopped in Dallas to spend the night, his pseudonym posed something of a problem since his baggage had not made the same flight he had.

"I stayed at the Adolphus Hotel under the name of Jim Pittman," Royal recalled. "But my airline ticket was in my name and so they had a heckuva time getting the bags to me; they sent them to the hotel for Darrell Royal. Actually, I don't think anyone would have recognized my name if they had put it up on the marquee at the Adolphus; nobody knew who Darrell Royal was, anyway."

That same night, Bible told his wife that he had to get up early the next morning because he was going to the airport to pick up "the next University of Texas football coach."

Royal detained Bible in the car before they went in to meet the Athletic Council, asking for a physical description of each member and for other information which might be helpful to him. When Bible mentioned that Lloyd Hand (who later became an aide to President

Lyndon B. Johnson) was the student representative on the council, Royal asked if he should address him as "Mr. Hand."

"No-o-o-o, Darrell," said Bible, in that deeply resonant voice, "I believe it would be proper to address him as just 'Lloyd.'"

Perhaps it was such thorough "scouting" and preparation by Royal that made his trip to Austin so successful so quickly. After visiting with the council, he was taken to see Dr. Logan Wilson, the president of the university, and from there to the Commodore Perry Hotel for a visit with the Board of Regents.

"They asked me all sorts of questions—such as what kind of salary I'd expect, what size staff I thought I'd need, and if I believed in working out on Sundays. I'm sure they threw in some questions not because they cared about the answers but just to see how I'd react."

What did he say when asked about the salary?

"I told 'em that, really, I'd like to have a decent salary but that was not the most important thing to me. The important thing was having a job with the chance to succeed, and having it set up so that I didn't have any blind alleys—so that I could have open communication with other people at the University. That opened up an opportunity for me to talk about these things—and I really wasn't answering their question on what I thought I ought to have in salary.

"After all that, they got back to the salary and I told them, 'Just don't embarrass me and ask me to come for nothing.' They'd been talking to coaches who were asking for the moon. I knew that, and this was a direct switch. I was making seventeen thousand dollars a year. They hired me at seventeen. But then they decided they ought to give me at least a little raise, so they made it seventeen-five, with a five-year contract.

"They had also asked me about the athletics directorship. Now, I know they're not going to give me the directorship at age thirty-two. But I also don't want to deal myself out for the future; I want to leave the door open. So I said, 'Well, I really think I would be too busy as football coach to handle any directorship duties and I don't want to be saddled with that; I want to be free to get this football program going.'

"I knew that was the main thing they wanted, but I also felt that way. I wasn't lighting a shuck with them; I wasn't being deceitful or misleading, because I really felt that way. I went on and said, 'If, after about five years, my work has been satisfactory to you people, I'd like to be considered for director of athletics.' I didn't know it then but this fit the picture perfectly because that five years would just about hit Ed Olle's retirement. They didn't want to make me athletics director until they'd looked at me for a while but this gave me an opportunity to hang onto that possibility."

Olle had been, for many years, the business manager of athletics at the University, where he had starred in baseball. He had a lot of strong support for promotion to director of athletics.

Royal's answers all seemed to be right. He was in Austin less than four hours before everyone involved, including the regents, decided he was the man they wanted for football coach; Olle would be named director of athletics.

"Just before noon, the regents shooed me outside so they could make their final decision, " said Royal, "but I felt then that I had the job. As a matter of fact, I found a phone and called Edith to tell her I was getting it . . . ."

By that time, Pittman and Campbell were practically on the road to Texas. By the time Royal got back to Seattle, they were.

"We moved almost that fast, just because we were so anxious to get closer to home," said Royal. "When I got back to Seattle, Edith already had the moving van there, and things boxed up. We didn't even have any place to sit.

"We had a beautiful house out there, with a wonderful location. We were right on Lake Washington and we could sit out there and watch the crews practicing. We could look across the lake and right into the football stadium. We were almost within walking distance of the campus. And the scenery out there is the prettiest I've ever seen, anywhere.

"I really liked living out there and I liked the people there, but it was just too far from home. We had three kids and if we'd come back to Oklahoma, the only way we could make it in our allotted vacation time was to fly. And if I flew my family back to visit the relatives, it would take everything I'd made in a year just to spend a couple of weeks at home.

"It's just so far from where I grew up, and where our relatives were. You know, Seattle's right up there in the corner; there's nobody 'going through' Seattle. In Austin, I catch a lot of my friends going through here to some other place, and have a chance to visit with them. Man, you're not going anywhere when you go through Seattle ; you're out in the ocean or up in Canada."

It seems a little ironic that there were almost as many objections when Royal left Seattle, after one year, as there had been when he arrived.

Will Connolly wrote a sports column for the *San Francisco Chronicle* that was especially critical of Royal's leaving three years on a four-year contract to take the Texas job.

"He goes where the most money is tomorrow and where best working conditions obtain, without regard to written agreements," said Connolly.

Royal recalls that "some of the people were kinda howling about me leaving and coming to Texas."

"I just asked 'em to check the record and see what had happened to all the other coaches that had been there during the past forty years; I was the only one to leave voluntarily. All the others were fired. Coaching out there was a wonderful experience for me and all the people were very nice to us. But I didn't have any trouble at all making up my mind to come to Texas."

Royal was so anxious to reach Texas that when he and his family left their house in Seattle, he forgot to put Edith's suitcase in the car.

"That night, we stopped somewhere about five hundred miles down the road, and that's when we realized that I'd left her clothes in Seattle," said Royal. "We'd told the movers to pick up everything we'd left but all Edith had with her was some sweaters and blue jeans she had brought to wear in the car. We were gonna leave the kids in Oklahoma and go to the Cotton Bowl Game. That's what we did, but Edith had to buy a bunch of new clothes when we got to Dallas, so she could go to the parties there.

"The kids were all excited about moving to Texas," said Royal, recalling that Marian then was eleven, Mack was nine and David four.

"We surprised them," said Royal, "because they'd really been wanting to go to Disneyland. I wanted to get on to Texas but we decided we oughta go down there and spend a day and a night there. I remember how excited they were. They enjoyed it so much; and I had such a good time, seeing them so happy. I remember how excited Marian was—"

By the time the Royals finished their Disneyland visit, Darrell could hardly wait to get to Texas. As a matter of fact, he was in such a hurry that he got a speeding ticket in New Mexico.

"I handed the patrolman my driver's license,"said Royal, "and he wrote out the ticket. Then, as he handed it to me, he said: 'Well, Mr. Royal, if you can get that Texas football team to run as fast as you drive, you'll do all right.'

"I was really thrilled because he knew who I was. Nothing like that had ever happened to me before and I was so flattered that I really didn't mind too much going into town and paying a fifteen-dollar fine . . . ."

After enjoying first-class treatment during the Cotton Bowl festivities, which were climaxed by TCU's nosing out Syracuse, 28-27, Royal was shocked to see the facilities which greeted him at the University of Texas.

His office was a small cubicle, about eight feet square, equipped with an old steel desk and a straight-back chair held together with adhesive tape. He had no secretary or receptionist.

"If the phone rings, I've got to answer it, no matter who I'm visiting with," said Royal. "If anybody wants to see me, they just walk through the door—and it doesn't matter who I've got in my office. If I'm sitting there trying to have a private conversation with someone, I've got telephone calls, I've got interruptions, I've got people coming in and out—it's enough to give you hives.

"I couldn't recruit, I couldn't talk to a sportswriter, I couldn't talk to an alumnus—I couldn't talk privately to anybody in my office. I'd have to get up and leave the office to have a private conversation with anyone. And when I did that, my phone would ring and I couldn't even get the messages. You talk about being frustrated: you can't have a private conversation in your own office and if you leave your office you'll miss some phone calls you shouldn't be missing . . . .

"Besides that, the locker room hadn't been painted in about twenty years and the walls of the showers were slimy. The practice field was full of goatheads. And they watered the field just by trying to move a hose around. The office setup wasn't adequate at all. As a matter of fact, all the assistant coaches were in one room and there was no way any of them could work in there. About all they could do was sit around and shoot the bull because when one guy would try to work, the others would be laughing and talking and kidding . . . .

"Our coaching staff began complaining about the situation, after we had been here a while, and they were all pretty dejected. I finally called them in and told them that if everything had been the way it should be here, Texas probably would have won more than just one game the year before and we might not be here. I told 'em that all these things actually were pluses for us because they were things that could be corrected, but it would take some time because you can't change these things overnight.

"Of course, I tried to change them as quickly as I could. I'm sure that, at the age of thirty-two, and as aggressive as I was, I must have irritated Mr. Bible and Mr. Olle quite a bit. I tried not to but I know I did, because their faces would get flushed every now and then when I'd ask 'em when I was gonna get this and when I was gonna get that."

The first significant break-through on this front, as far as Royal was concerned, came when he managed to get his tiny office partitioned off. Mrs. Blanche Rhodes, who was secretary for the entire coaching staff, then moved into Royal's outer office and managed to help organize the parade of people trying to talk with him.

"Then we reworked the practice field completely," said Royal. "We had it poisoned and plowed up, to kill those stickers, and we got some good grass from A&M and had a sprinkler system installed. Then the guys could get down there and work on blocking and tackling without getting their hands and arms and knees full of stickers . . . ."

Royal had no contact with Ed Price, his predecessor who had gone into University administration, when he first came to Texas.

"But I sincerely believe that he is a good enough man that he was pulling for me to do well, just because he loves the University of Texas," said Royal. "And I'm sure that, coming in fresh, I was able to get some things done that he couldn't have—even though he may have wanted the same things done."

A great many changes in the physical appearance of UT athletic facilities—and Longhorn athletes—have evolved naturally and, in Royal's opinion, would have done so regardless of who was coaching the football team.

But it obviously took a great deal of success on the football field to make possible the expansion, completed in 1972, of Memorial Stadium to its present seating capacity of 80,000. A 15,000-seat, upper deck cantilever added to the west side juts out from the top of a seven-story building constructed adjacent to the grandstand.

The building supporting that upper deck houses first class offices for the Department of Athletics along with the Physical Education Department, laboratories, gymnasiums, handball and squash courts, and headquarters for the campus police. Two high-speed escalators and four elevators help handle traffic to and from the upper deck of the stadium.

There is little resemblance to the original Memorial Stadium, completed in 1924, nor to its appearance when Royal arrived in 1957. But the physical appearance of Longhorn athletes probably has changed even more drastically than that of the stadium during Royal's tenure at Texas, especially when it comes to hair styles. Similar changes have taken place at other schools, of course, but Royal is one coach whom the longer hair doesn't bother at all.

"It was just a natural thing when I came to Texas," he said, "for the athletes to wear crew-cuts. That was the 'in-thing.' The 'in-thing' now is *not* to have a crew-cut. They like a mustache, they like longer hair, they like to be like the rest of the students.

"Back in 1957, I didn't tell anybody they had to get a crew-cut, anymore than I tell them now they can't wear their hair long. Back at that time, you never did tell anybody what they could do or couldn't do about their hair. They just naturally did it, just like they just naturally do what they want to do now.

"I'm still strong," said Royal, "on all the points I think you have to be strong in, on points that are reasonable—such as being on time at practice and at meetings, being dressed in what I consider acceptable fashion when we're traveling, conduct in the hotel lobby, and in the rooms, and off the field, and out of season; these things haven't changed any.

"You still have to have pride in your appearance as a team—and in your performance as a team."

When he first came to Texas, Royal regarded the task of instilling pride in the football program as one of his most formidable challenges. He felt confident he could do so among the players but he knew that alone would not be enough. And when it came to trying to "sell" the faculty, football fans and the general public on his ideas, he had some serious doubts about his own ability; despite the silver-tongued persuasiveness he had utilized to win the Texas job, he still was haunted by the belief that he was a poor public speaker.

Except, he felt, on the football field and in the locker room . . . .

Chapter 9

A SILVER TONGUE

During his first year at Texas, Royal made it a point to stay away from "people downtown" and from others who wanted to tell him what had been wrong with the UT football program. When someone cornered him on that subject, he would listen as long as he had to—and be as noncommittal as possible.

But he immediately sought out suggestions and advice in another field, public speaking, from an expert.

"I contacted my good friend, Bill Alexander, who was pastor of the First Christian Church in Oklahoma City," said Royal. "He was one of the all time gifted after-dinner speakers. He was a showman—he was show biz—and boy, could he talk! I mean he was some super speaker. I went to Oklahoma City and spent some time with him, talking to him about nothing but speaking."

Alexander gave Royal a short poem, entitled "The Bridge," and told him to memorize it one afternoon.

"I'm going to pick you up tonight and take you out to the house and listen to you say it," the famed evangelist told him. "And I'm going to cut you up. You're my friend and I'm trying to help you. You did come up here to be helped, didn't you?"

Royal replied affirmatively, then spent the afternoon working on the poem. That evening, Alexander and his wife, Mickey, settled down to listen. But Royal wasn't more than halfway through the poem when Alexander stopped him and mocked: "Da-*da*, da-*da*, da-*da*, da-*da*—no wonder you shouldn't use poems! No one should use poems if they're going to sing-song them. You're supposed to be telling a story. The poem tells a story so use it the same way you'd tell a story."

Then Alexander got up and started walking around the room, telling the story of the poem to a spellbound Royal.

When Darrell left Oklahoma City, Alexander urged him to keep working on the poem and to call him and recite it over the telephone when he thought he had it right. It took several calls before Royal rang the bell.

Finally, one day Royal phoned from Amarillo and began reciting the poem. After a few lines, Alexander interrupted by calling to his wife: "Mickey! Pick up the extension phone; I think he's got it!"

Royal eventually realized that the same technique he used so successfully with football players would work just as well with other crowds—and that is something he sums up simply as "just being your natural self."

"I've never tried to pattern myself after anyone," he said. "I've just tried to be me. I've always thought it was a big mistake for a guy to try to imitate his own coach, and use his mannerisms. Your natural self has to reflect the people you've been around, and so they *do* influence you. But if you try to imitate them, it's phony.

"Sometimes, I have nothing at all to say in the locker room. Sometimes, I might get wound up and talk five or ten minutes. But I just do what's natural and I don't do many things that are premeditated.

"I kinda live one day at a time, and scratch where it itches. If I'm upset about something, I usually express it. If I'm elated and pleased about something, I usually express that to the team, and visit with them about it. But I have never tried to invent emotions. If the emotion is there, and it's there naturally, I've never tried to suppress it or hide it; but if it's not there, I've never tried to invent it.

"Sometimes, I've been so emotional and choked up I could hardly talk, but there have been a lot of other times when I didn't feel that way at all. So I just do what's natural, and whatever I feel. Looking back on it, I think that's the way most of the coaches who coached me felt."

Royal insists that he cannot recall ever making a speech at halftime which he thought turned a game around but many observers believe he is simply being too modest in that regard.

"I'm not that much of a speaker, to begin with," he contends. "And I think you've got to be a talented, gifted speaker to do that. I do think that if you're sincere, even in a clumsy way, sometimes it might have some effect.

"Usually, the better the job we've done preparing for a game, the less I've had to do at halftime. When you're best prepared, you have the least to say."

Among those who have been shocked at how little he usually has to say in the locker room are the "guest coaches." The first year he was at Texas, Royal began inviting three faculty members to spend the weekend with the team for each home game. Later, he began inviting three non-faculty fans to do the same thing on out-of-town games—to attend all team meetings, eat with the team, join it in the locker room and sit on the bench during the game.

"I thought this was a good idea because there are so many misconceptions about what a football program is—what we're doing, what we're teaching, the way we go about it. If football is good, and is a part of our educational system, and we should have it on the campus, then our faculty should be informed about what we're doing.

"We don't do anything to try to impress the guest coaches. All we do is invite them to come in and see what we're doing. They're usually surprised at how little we say in the locker room before a game. But if you're going to put a big story on the players at that time, you sure have held it back a long time. It takes steady input and steady progress throughout the week to get ready for a ball game."

Royal was not at all convinced that the input and progress had been steady enough when he took his first Texas team to Atlanta for its season-opener with Georgia on September 21, 1957.

"I've always been nervous before opening games, but I was scared to death before that one," he recalled. "I couldn't tell whether we were ready for major competition or not."

He still wasn't sure even when that game ended, since Georgia miscues contributed significantly to Texas' 26-7 victory. Still, Texas looked promising in taking advantage of Georgia fumbles and penalties.

Quarterback Walter Fondren did guide the Longhorns impressively on a 60-yard touchdown march. Then, too, they gained 226 yards rushing—which was about as pleasing to Royal as anything other than the final score.

The more he thought about it, the more pleasing it seemed. And by the time he spoke at a Longhorn Club luncheon the following Wednesday, he had found a great many things in the game movie to which he could point with pride.

"I remember leaving that meeting and wondering if I hadn't been a little too positive about the way I thought football ought to be coached," said Royal. "I was so damned proud of that victory and I was showing them some of the things our team was doing well. I thought it might have sounded like I was bragging too much, I was so elated."

"Damned" is a word which did not seem to be a part of his personal vocabulary at the time. His strongest expletives in those days ran to "Golly Ned!" and "Gosh-all-Friday!"

Profanity or not, his choice of words was superb when he faced the Longhorns in the locker room at College Station on Thanksgiving Day, just before they finished their regular season with the traditional grudge game against Texas A&M. They had won five games, lost three and tied one—and were still in the running for the Southwest Conference championship (although a Texas victory over A&M would have had to be combined with a Baylor upset of Rice the following Saturday to put the Longhorns in the Cotton Bowl).

The Sugar Bowl officials had made it clear that they wanted the winner of the A&M-Texas game to face Mississippi in the 1958 Sugar Bowl Classic. The Aggies, being coached by Bear Bryant for the last time before his return to Alabama, were favored by eight points in the nationally-televised game.

A year earlier, A&M had beaten Texas in Austin for the first time since 1924—putting the clincher on that 1-9 season.

Now, as they prepared for their last regular season game, Royal singled out the seniors who had been so maligned the previous year. He praised them for their dedication and leadership and for helping to get the Longhorn football back on the winning track.

By the time he asked the seniors to line up by the door, there wasn't a dry eye in the locker room. Then he told the rest of the squad, in a voice choked with emotion: "I want every one of you to go by and shake the hands of these men—and then go out there and beat those Aggies!"

Pittman, the offensive line coach, remarked several years later that he had never seen any team so fired up.

"They practically fought each other trying to get over there to those seniors," he said.

On the second play of the game, Fondren quick-kicked 62 yards and the ball died on the A&M 4. A 22-yard Aggie punt a few moments later gave Texas the ball on the A&M 33. Eight plays later, Quarterback Bobby Lackey dived into the end zone from a yard out for the Longhorns' only touchdown.

Lackey kicked a 38-yard field goal during the third quarter to make it Texas 9, A&M 0. But the Aggies came storming back, aided by a 57-yard pass from Roddy Osborne to All-America John Crow, in the fourth quarter. The Longhorns used up seven minutes driving from their own 20 to the Aggie 46 following that touchdown but still had to intercept a couple of passes to ice down the 9-7 victory.

It was the sweetest win, said Royal, of his coaching career up to that point. It was followed by one of the worst defeats—a 39-7 shellacking by Ole Miss in the Sugar Bowl. But Royal still believes his Longhorns deserved a far better fate on that trip to New Orleans.

"We really didn't have a team of bowl caliber," he admitted later. "And it might have been better for us, in the long run, to get deflated the way we did since we'd done so much better during the regular season than anybody had expected us to do."

Royal decided that he had worked his squad too hard for the Ole Miss game, partly because he regarded extending the season for an extra month to be what amounted to an "extra" spring practice. He learned from that mistake, however, and altered his bowl game practice schedules considerably after that.

"But we really weren't as poorly prepared for the Ole Miss game as it looked like we were," he said. "For instance, we had Raymond Brown nailed back there in their end zone when he got a bad pass from center on fourth down. We've got the kick blocked, but he picks up the ball and turns it into a ninety-two yard touchdown run. Those things just happen."

And they happen, he feels, regardless of what is said in the locker room.

"If you have the best personnel and you get the breaks, you win," Royal believes. "It's that simple. I've never felt that we've 'out-coached' anybody. I'm just not one who believes football coaches can 'out-think' or 'out-talk' each other. And they all work as hard as we do here."

Those who have played for Royal tend to agree that he never makes what would be considered an old-fashioned "pep talk." But they also are inclined, under prodding, to recall instances in which he has used just a few choice words most effectively and fired the team up to fever pitch.

"I've made a conscientious effort to stay away from that phony psychological stuff," says Royal. "If I tried to 'bull' my players, they'd pick it up in a minute. They can read me like a book, anyway.

"Why, just the other day, one of them walked up to me and, before I'd even said a word, he said, 'Coach, I can tell you're miffed . . . .' He was right, too. I sure was.

"Football is a physical contact, spartan game. You don't go out there for any taffy-pull, so you'd better have your emotions running pretty high when you get on that field. But I can't work up a 'hate campaign' against someone I don't hate.

"I never say anything unless I feel motivated and unless I really believe what I'm saying. But one of the things that is so fascinating to me about coaching is deciding what I'm going to say to the squad—not just before a game, but from day to day.

"For instance, if a boy lets down and does a lousy job, should you chew him out? Or would it be better to give him a pat on the back and encourage him to do better next time?

"Coaching is largely a matter of dealing with people, and it's a new world every day. I never feel like I'm going to work when I get up in the morning. It's a wonderful profession when you can earn a livelihood and not feel like you're working to do it.

"The only thing that really disturbs me about my profession is the fact that people give you too much credit when you win and too much criticism when you lose. I'll be the same person and do the same things and say the same things when we lose, but people won't believe me then. I won't change, but the people will.

"But if a coach could set up the ideal situation, I doubt that I'd be happy with what I picked," he added. "You've got to have a challenge. How can you truly appreciate a compliment if you've never been criticized?"

For Royal, the challenge is there—every Saturday during the football season.

"I'm the world's biggest coward," he said once. "I run scared all the time. I agree with President Eisenhower: just before the election, the opposition always looks twelve feet tall."

While he might profess a lack of courage and speaking ability, the evidence indicates that Royal usually appears to about "twelve feet tall" to his own players. For example, Carlos D. Conde, then sports editor of *The Daily Texan*, the UT campus newspaper, wrote in 1959:

"We're sure glad Darrell Royal decided to be a coach and not a professional soldier. If he could fire up an army before a battle like he does his players before a game, he would be our modern-day Napoleon without ever having to scratch his chest.

"Royal in his own bailiwick is like Billy Graham before his own congregation. A master of words, he uses a different text to approach football's hour of decision, but the attention he commands and the response he receives from his devotees parallels that of Graham.

"Not only is he a prolific speaker with an articulate voice and effective mannerisms, but his locker room speeches are rarely the same. He's not the coach with the stereotype pep talk that has the "Gee-fellows-have-a-heart-I-have-a-wife-and-three-kids-to-feed " appeal.

"We were introduced to these talks as a student equipment manager in 1957 and though our role was small, his words nevertheless left us with a feverish desire to walk across the field and slam the opposing team's manager with our water buckets . . . ."

Royal always has realized that what he said to outsiders, such as luncheon clubs, also was being said to his squad. When he talked to the Longhorn Club a few days before the 1958 Oklahoma game, he acknowledged that the Sooners were favored by 13 points but declared, "I think we can win."

"The only way anybody's going to beat Oklahoma is to go out there and whip 'em jaw to jaw," he said. "They get a yellow dog running downhill and they'll strap him real good. The thing I want to see is that they earn what they get with some bumps and bruises.

"Texas has to develop a football tradition," he declared. "It had one once, but lost it. When we get one, maybe we can stop that blood-letting up at Dallas and turn it into a good show."

Oklahoma had beaten Texas six times straight, at that point, and nine times during the last 10 games. Thus, when the Longhorns came from behind to upset the Sooners, 15-14, pandemonium reigned—even when the Longhorns' chartered plane tried to land at the Austin Municipal Airport several hours later.

"That was one of the most important victories we've had," said Royal. "And the fans didn't leave any doubt about their thinking it was. The plane couldn't even land because of all the fans at the airport. That was when we had that old terminal building, and I remember looking out of the plane and seeing people swarming all over it, just like ants. It gave you a big thrill. And it was a new experience for the players but I felt that they'd really earned it . . . ."

From a historical standpoint, it may be tragic that many of Royal's pregame and halftime comments have not been recorded for posterity. But it may also be that the resultant mystery enhances the facts. During the 1967 Texas-Oklahoma game, for instance, the Sooners all but crucified the Longhorns during the first half—and still wound up with only a 7-0 lead at the intermission. Texas dominated the second half completely and walked off with a 9-7 victory which knocked Oklahoma out of a national championship.

Among the sportswriters covering that game was Bill Van Fleet of the *Fort Worth Star-Telegram*, a man who commanded great respect from football coaches as well as from his fellow newsmen. As he started to leave the press box that night, Van Fleet turned and told a friend:

"I don't have any idea what Darrell told his team at halftime today. But some Monday morning when I've got a hangover and don't want to get up and go to work, when I'd just as soon lie there and maybe die, I just wish he'd walk into my bedroom and tell me the same thing he told them."

The main thing Royal's players remembered about his halftime remarks that day was the admonition, delivered rather heatedly, that "There's a helluva fight going on out there—*by one side*. Why don't you get in on it?"

(Photo by Rick Henson)
Royal and his longtime friend, Willie Nelson, visit during a 1991 golf tournament.

Chapter 10

POWER AND THE PRESS

The late—and great—Bill Van Fleet, a kind and gentle person who never wanted to hurt anyone, may have been the epitome of sportswriters who tried to do their jobs and level with the readers while not taking undue advantage of the coaches or raking them over the coals unnecessarily.

It took Royal quite a while, after he came to Texas, to realize that such sportswriters even existed. He was inclined, at first, to think that every writer either was "for" him or "against" him. He took offense at many questions which were aimed merely at gaining information, because he felt they implied criticism. And he answered those, frequently, with biting sarcasm.

"I was wearing my feelings on my sleeve those first few years at Texas," he admits.

After winning 13-12 squeakers from both Arkansas and Baylor in 1959, Texas went into the TCU game with an 8-0 record. It was the first time since 1941 for the Longhorns to risk an undefeated record against TCU, an old spoiler.

Snow and sleet set the stage for that memorable clash in Memorial Stadium in Austin. When the canvas cover was taken off the field shortly before game time, the sleet which had covered it was piled up on the sidelines. Officially, the temperature was 31 degrees at kickoff time, with a cold north wind whipping through the big horseshoe; unofficially, the chill factor varied back and forth between "miserable" and "unbearable."

Several bales of hay were scattered in front of each bench to provide insulation from the sleet, which began to melt and turn to slush during the game. The bitter cold kept the bands from marching at halftime. And when Bevo, the longhorn steer which serves as the Texas mascot, came out of his trailer just before the game, he balked immediately and tried to get back into it.

Texas held a 9-0 lead at halftime but TCU slashed back during the third quarter and cut that to 9-7. Then, midway through the fourth quarter, a second-team back named Harry Moreland slipped through a hole at right tackle and went 56 yards to give the Frogs a 14-9 upset victory, one of the most memorable in TCU history.

In the locker room after the game, sportswriters groping for "inside" information which might not have been apparent to the fans asked Royal about the effects of the unusually cold weather. One noted that the Frogs wore long-sleeved jerseys and high stockings, then covered their legs with a long strip of plastic while sitting on the bench, but the Longhorns took no such precautions. When he was asked if the short-sleeved jerseys might have bothered his players, Royal snapped: "I guess somebody will fault us for that—playing in short sleeves. But when they come off that field sweating, the cold weather is not bothering them."

A few days later, the *San Antonio Express* published an article saying there were rumors that Royal and Quarterback Bobby Lackey had quarreled at halftime. Royal, who still insists those rumors were totally false, slashed back at the time by declaring: "After winning eight straight, suddenly the players are out of shape, there's dissension on the club and we're under-clad."

Actually, Royal felt that TCU had excellent personnel that year and that it was a shame the Horned Frogs did not play all season the way they played against Texas. That feeling led to a widely-misunderstood quote from him, which has been used ever since to fire up TCU teams.

"They're like a bunch of cockroaches," Royal said of the Frogs. "It's not what they eat and tote off—it's what they fall into and mess up that hurts."

Years later, Royal reflected on that statement and commented: "All I was trying to say is that you wallow around with all this ability, and you don't go for the championship; you just want to mess up something for somebody else. I felt that TCU should have been trying to go to the Cotton Bowl that year. They were good enough; they had great personnel. But all they were interested in was keeping somebody else from going."

It was about that time that Bud Shrake, then a sportswriter for *The Dallas Morning News* and later an associate editor of *Sports Illustrated*, blew his top because Royal failed to return until Thursday a telephone call Shrake placed to him on Monday; in fact, Shrake had replaced the call on Tuesday, Wednesday and Thursday.

When Royal finally called back, Shrake complained bitterly.

"Well, you just don't understand how much all these calls interfere with my schedule," said Royal. "And besides, I get tired of going back over the same things all the time with you writers."

"Well, let me tell you something," said Shrake. "You're not doing much for my schedule, either. And the answers you guys give kinda put me to sleep, too. I don't care what you've told anybody else—and I really don't much care, at this point, what you tell me. But my bosses have told me that I have to get certain questions answered. I couldn't care less how you answer them. Frankly, your answers bore me to death. But I've got to get 'em, regardless of how boring they are . . . ."

Royal said he learned a valuable lesson from that conversation.

"The thought suddenly occurred to me that he was right, that he had a job to do, and he really was helping me to do my job," said Royal. "I figured that we had to work together, even though he didn't like it any better than I did. He wasn't thrilled about talking to me any more than I was thrilled about talking to him. But we've both got a job to do and we can both do it better by working with each other.

"That's why I really try hard now, when I'm talking to someone from the press, to give him something he can write. It's very easy to sit there and not use any imagination, and just give 'em routine, middle-of-the-road answers to their questions. And then the poor guy's sitting there without anything to work with, but he's still got a job to do. And he's got a 'dud' as a subject to write about.

"Even if I've gone right over the same material with someone else, I try—if I possibly can—to give each writer some fresh kind of slant, or new angle, even on the same subject. I just kinda feel that if I work with a writer and try to help him, he's going to be more inclined to help me later on if I need help."

Royal is the first to admit that it took some time for him to develop that attitude. And he gives a large amount of the credit for it to former Gov. Allan Shivers, who talked him out of making a grave mistake in 1962.

The Longhorns were riding high in midseason that year. After trouncing Oregon, Texas Tech and Tulane, they nosed out Oklahoma, 9-6, and then won a spine-tingling, 7-3 thriller from Arkansas in Austin.

Arkansas held a 3-0 lead in the third quarter when it launched a long drive which gave the Porkers a first down on the Longhorn 5-yard line. That's when Texas Linebacker Johnny Treadwell delivered one of the most famous orations in UT football annals.

"Okay," Treadwell told his teammates at that point. "We've got 'em right where we want 'em now. They've run out of room. They can't throw a long pass—they've got to come right at us!"

Two plays later, with Arkansas facing third down on the Texas 3, Linebackers Treadwell and Pat Culpepper jarred Razorback Fullback Danny Brabham loose from the ball. Texas' Joe Dixon recovered it in the end zone for a touchback.

That gave Texas the breath of life it needed. Midway of the fourth period, the Longhorns launched a 90-yard, 20-play drive. Quarterback Duke Carlisle initiated it but, exhausted after playing both offense and defense for most of the game, turned the controls over to Johnny Genung at midfield.

Several times that drive seemed likely to stall; twice the Longhorns had to convert fourth-down situations into first downs. Periodically, after Texas passed midfield, Royal called for Tony Crosby, his place-kicking specialist. Every time he did, some of the Longhorns on the bench would moan or even yell, "Oh, no!"

"Sure, I heard 'em," Royal said later. "I didn't want to settle for a field goal either but I wanted Crosby ready in case we needed him. I didn't want to have to take a five-yard penalty looking for him, if we needed him, and force him to kick it five yards further. I was looking ahead, just in case."

Tommy Ford finally slammed his way over the goal line from four yards out, just 36 seconds before the game ended. Crosby's extra-point kick made the final score Texas 7, Arkansas 3.

That sent the Longhorns marching into their clash with Rice the next week riding a 5-0 record. And that's when much of the sugar suddenly turned to salt. With the score Texas 14, Rice 14, in the fourth quarter, the Longhorns twice faced fourth-down situations in midfield, needing only about a yard for a first down each time. Both times, Royal ordered punts. When the game ended in a 14-14 tie, these decisions brought him a great deal of criticism.

"One of those punts hit one of our guys, who was going down to cover it, on the heel and bounced back twenty-five yards," Royal recalled, many years later. "If I'd known it was going to hit his heel and bounce back, I wouldn't have wanted to kick, either. But I felt then that was the best opportunity we had to win the game, and I still feel that way.

"But I also feel that the people who disagreed with me had a point, because it was delicate—whether you should go for it or punt. I'm still not firmly convinced that punting was the *only* thing to do. It was debatable. And I debated it in my mind before I decided to kick."

Royal feels much more generous toward those critics now than he did at the time. Much of the criticism came from Lou Maysel, the mild-mannered sports editor of the *Austin American-Statesman* who later wrote the excellent history on University of Texas football, *Here Come the Texas Longhorns*.

Maysel's comments about the Rice game were so critical that Royal seriously considered barring him from the practice field and the locker room. Leonard Smith, Shivers' airplane pilot and a close friend of the Longhorn coaches, learned of this and relayed the information to his boss. Shivers promptly called Royal and asked him not to do anything about it until they had a chance to discuss the matter.

That night, which happened to be Halloween, Darrell and Edith rang the doorbell at the Shivers' residence, the Pease Mansion in Austin. Shivers went to the door, thinking he would be greeted by some more "trick-or-treaters." When he saw the Royals, he laughed and said, "Trick or treat!"

Royal managed a smile as he replied, "I hope it's a treat; I want to talk with you."

They got down to business pretty quickly, with Royal telling the former governor exactly how he felt.

"Let's assume that you're right," said Shivers. "Even if you are, there's no way you could come out ahead by doing this, so you'd still be making a terrible mistake. Not only would you make Lou mad, but you'd make a lot of other sportswriters mad at you, too. When you're in a position as prominent as you are and have to deal with the press all the time, there's no way you can win a running battle with the press."

Royal believed him—and took his advice to heart.

"It was through Governor Shivers' guidance and advice that I pulled back, for which I'll always be thankful," said Royal. "Lou has been an extremely fair writer. That's the only time he's really taken exception to anything I've done—and he had a side. He was very critical about that fourteen-to-fourteen tie with Rice, and that was his prerogative. It was questionable, whether we kick or don't kick. It was about fifty-fifty. You take either side; the side we took just didn't pan out.

"Lou has been fair and we've had a good relationship. It would have been a terrible mistake for me, because I had my feelings on my sleeve, to go tell him off and make a lifelong enemy out of him. He really has become a good friend, and a good friend of the program. I don't think he's a 'Homer Joe,' by any means, but I think he's fair.

"I'm certainly not without mistakes. And when some guy sees that and wants to write about it, and does write about it, I really can't complain—because they put it up there pretty good when we do something good. Governor Shivers' advice was excellent; I not only followed it in that particular case, but also adopted it as a general rule.

"I still don't like criticism. But I can stand it a lot easier now than I could then. When some guy gigs me, I look back and say, 'Well, has he written some favorable stuff about me?' And I say, 'Yes.' Then I say, 'Well, has he written more favorable stuff than unfavorable stuff?' And I have to say, 'Yes.' Well, those are pretty good odds.

"I thought I made some bad statements on the George Sauer incident," said Royal, "and I called Red Smith and told him I had. I'd made the statement that we had 'wet-nursed' Sauer and brought him along to the right spot and then he was gone.

"Sauer made a clever reply. He said, 'If you call all those blocking and tackling drills I went through wet-nursing, I guess he did.' We didn't wet-nurse him. We didn't mistreat him but we didn't wet-nurse him, either. And I think we helped George Sauer as a football player."

Sauer, who caught a 69-yard touchdown pass that helped Texas upset Alabama, 21-17, in the 1965 Orange Bowl Game, passed up his final year of collegiate eligibility to join the New York Jets. That provoked some bitter words from Royal.

"But I never did blame George," said Royal. "Weeb Ewbank (of the Jets) told me they wanted to come watch practice when we were working out for the Orange Bowl. He assured me they wouldn't try to take any of our players. I opened up practice to them and it caused them to take a boy who still had eligibility left.

"Of course, it was George's privilege to leave. He could have left after the first year, the second year or the third year. Or the first day. He's not obligated to stay here and finish out his time and I never did feel that he was. So it wasn't George that I was upset with."

While many writers have become upset with Royal from time to time, they generally find it difficult to maintain any sort of ill feeling toward him. And one of the main reasons for that undoubtedly is the fact that he is cooperative.

He started holding Monday noon press conferences when he first came to Texas, at the suggestion of Wilbur Evans, who was then sports information director at Texas and later became executive vice president and general manager of the Cotton Bowl Classic. Then, under the guidance of Jones Ramsey, who succeeded Evans at Texas, he also began holding post-mortem sessions with sportswriters after each game—always giving the writers a couple of hours to file their game stories before meeting with them to rehash the day's events for their future columns.

It was during Ramsey's first year, 1961, that Royal first showed signs of mellowing in his attitude toward the press. A group of sportswriters discussed this one night during midseason, while Texas was rolling along undefeated. In earlier seasons, they noted, Royal's sarcastic answers frequently had made perfectly logical questions sound stupid. Now, it seemed, he was displaying a lot of patience in answering even the questions which truly were stupid.

"It may be just because he's winning 'em all now," one veteran writer observed, "but it's amazing how much football all us sportswriters have learned since last year!"

That was the year Royal attracted national attention by introducing his "Flip-Flop" offense, which he contends did little more than simplify the players' assignments and thus help eliminate confusion. It also helped eliminate nine of Texas' 10 opponents and the Longhorns wound up with a 9-1 record, marred only by a 6-0 loss to TCU. Then they scored a memorable 12-7 victory over Mississippi in the Cotton Bowl on Jan. 1, 1962.

Royal's great record resulted in his being named the nation's "Coach of the Year" by the American Football Writers Association—an honor which, despite his highly impressive credentials, could not have been won without strong support from sportswriters in the Southwest.

The writers obviously were pleased by their improved relationship with Royal and were happy to let bygones be bygones. They are not inclined to hold a grudge against any news source who has discovered the value of cooperating with them—especially when that source takes ribbing as well as Royal does.

At the 1963 College All-Star Game in Chicago, for instance, after Royal had received so much criticism for those fourth-down punts during the 1962 Rice game, he encountered Shrake. The two chatted amiably but Royal noticed that Shrake kept staring at his tie clasp, which featured the figure of a punter who obviously had just kicked the ball.

Finally, Royal asked Shrake why he was studying it so closely.

"I'm just trying to figure out," replied the inimitable Shrake, "whether it's second down and two or third down and two."

Royal led the resultant gale of laughter, obviously enjoying the joke as much as anyone.

It probably is more than coincidental that Royal's relations with the press, and his self-confidence, improved just about in direct proportion to his coaching success. As he gained experience in dealing with the press, he obviously also was gaining experience in dealing with other people, including players. And he contends that coaching football consists mainly of dealing with people.

He also acknowledges that today's goals, once attained, frequently turn into almost meaningless mementoes of yesteryear.

"I remember how important it was to me, when I was in college, to be All-Conference or All-America," said Royal. "Now, I look back on it, and it's really not that important. And I'm not as proud of it now as I was when I was in college.

"Like 'Coach of the Year.' That was a burning ambition of mine as a young coach. I just thought that, boy, if I could get one of those plaques on the wall . . . .

"But after it once happens to you, you realize that you're not all that much smarter or that much better than other coaches, and really, that you didn't even do that much better job than you did the year before. And then you come along and have a seven-three season—and you might have worked just as hard, made just as many good decisions and really done just as good a job but had a lot of injuries and other bad luck.

"So what you finally do is sit down and realize that you have to have a lot of good luck, you have to work hard and have things fall into place.

"Being 'Coach of the Year' is like a national championship. I don't think there is such a thing as a national champion—a 'best team in the country' that can stand up and say, 'We can lick anybody in the United States.' I don't think there is any coach who can ever jump up and say, 'I did a better job than anybody else in the nation.' I don't think anybody can say he's the best coach, or the best quarterback, or the best tackle in the United States. I just think it's an impossible thing to pick—and it's an honor that always goes to the winners.

"Winning is not easy, of course. It takes a lot of sacrifices, and a lot of talent—but it also takes a heckuva lot of luck, and a lot of people are involved in it" Royal declared. "The years that I've been picked as national 'Coach of the Year' I haven't felt that I coached any better, or worked any harder, or did any better job than I did in some other years when I wasn't even picked as 'Coach of the Year' in the Southwest Conference.

"Sure, I was thrilled when Harold Keith phoned me while I was at Oklahoma and told me I'd made All-America. But I never really popped any chest buttons about that. You want to keep going, you want to get as much as there is to be had, and go as far as you can go. My first ambition was to make the starting lineup. I'm proud and pleased that I managed to do that, and then go on from there, but I've tried not to be too impressed with myself.

"For one thing, you look around and see that other people have had as much to do with your success as you've had. I wouldn't have been any 'Coach of the Year' if I'd stayed at Mississippi State; I might not have even had a job. The University of Texas had to give me a chance—or at least a place like the University of Texas had to give me a chance. You've got to be in the right place at the right time and have the right people say the right things about you. You've got to have a chance to do your thing.

"And when you get the chance, you have to be ready. I do think that I've worked hard at my profession and I've learned it well. I've also been blessed with a lot of wonderful assistants and some good football players and a great school. I haven't flubbed the opportunity but I still know that if I'd been at some other schools, I never would have been sitting on the top of the heap."

Royal recalled an exchange which took place once between Harold Ratliff, for many years the Associated Press sports editor in Texas who was noted for his needling questions, and Bear Bryant, while Bryant was coaching at A&M.

"Bear," Ratliff asked Bryant one night after an Aggie victory, "do you think you're a genius?"

Bryant looked at Ratliff for a moment and then replied, "No, I don't think I'm a genius—but I think I'm a damned good football coach."

"I guess that's kind of the way I feel," said Royal.

A great many other people feel that way now—but when he first came to Texas, it took Royal a while to convince them.

Chapter 11

TRIUMPH AND TRAGEDY

Since Texas had lost nine of its ten games in 1956, most Longhorn fans felt that Royal had jerked a miracle out of his hat when he finished the 1957 regular season with six victories, three losses and a tie. So did Royal, actually. And even that humiliating 39-7 loss to Ole Miss in the Sugar Bowl failed to dim the hope that a new era had dawned.

A 7-3 record in 1958 fanned the flames of that hope. Then, in 1959, the Longhorns managed to tie Arkansas and TCU for the Southwest Conference championship; they posted a 9-1 record and won the host role in the Cotton Bowl for the first time since Jan. 1, 1953.

The opponent was Syracuse. The result was Syracuse 23, Texas 14—and near chaos. Syracuse, favored by 13 points, held a 15-0 lead at halftime, which arrived about 20 seconds after a flurry of fisticuffs.

Syracuse Quarterback Dave Sarette threw a long pass to Ken Ericson, who was dismantled by Bobby Gurwitz and Jack Collins near the goal line. Ericson fumbled over the end line. Meanwhile, back in midfield, several players from each side were bravely trading punches—without, of course, bothering to take off their armor, which was most difficult for any fist to penetrate.

The "debate" began when Syracuse Lineman Al Gerlick was accused by Umpire Judy Truelson of illegal use of the hands while blocking. Gerlick's spirited protest drew support from John Brown, a 220-pound Negro tackle—and that prompted Texas Tackle Larry Stephens to advise, "Keep your black ass out of it!"

Stephens' natural, inadvertent and non-malicious reference to color immediately became a cause célèbre after the game, and was interpreted by some as a "racist" remark. But if Brown had weighed a little more, it is just as likely that Stephens would have told him to keep his "fat" ass out of it. Stephens simply used the most obvious descriptive term, without stopping to think about racial overtones; as a matter of fact, he admitted later, if he had stopped to think at all, he probably would not have said anything.

Nevertheless, a great many Eastern sportswriters who were looking for excuses to condemn racial discrimination seized upon this incident and played it for all it was worth. They claimed, among other things, that the

Longhorns had played "dirty football" in their contacts with the Syracuse blacks. What all this was worth turned out to be not very much after Royal invited the world to view movies of everything that had transpired.

Largely as a result of the evidence on film, Syracuse Athletics Director Lew Andreas eventually issued a statement which said: "No member of the Syracuse University administration, nor any member of its coaching staff, has accused the Texas team of playing 'dirty football' in the Cotton Bowl Game. As far as we are concerned, it was a hard-fought, exciting contest."

Syracuse Coach Ben Schwartzwalder had voiced a great many complaints in connection with the game. Royal refused to comment on those complaints then, but years later ridiculed the idea that any racial prejudice was involved in that extra-curricular activity on the field.

"The whole thing was blown up out of proportion," he declared. "They had some of the blacks from the Syracuse team on the 'Today' show and that fanned the flames. It was kinda like a little brush fire that gets out of control. There really wasn't anything racial about it. We had played against blacks before and that was not an issue at all.

"But after the game, Schwartzwalder complained that the Dallas night clubs were segregated, and his black players had not been allowed to do this and they had not been allowed to do that. But he knew all that before the game and if he felt that strongly about it, he should have just said, 'Syracuse University declines the invitation to the Cotton Bowl.' I think he was right—but he shouldn't have come down here and *then* tried to make a big issue out of things he had agreed to do.

"What makes him wrong was agreeing to participate and then complaining about it. If he had declined the invitation, I could *really* admire him—because he was right. There *were* some bad things about this part of the country at that time, so far as segregation is concerned. We were as wrong and as guilty as we could be on that, no question about it.

"Ben and I are very good friends now, and I have a lot of respect for what he's done for college football. But I still say there wasn't anything racial about what happened on that field."

The furor died down before the 1960 season started but it had focused renewed national attention on Texas. Despite extensive losses via graduation, the Longhorns were picked fourth in the Associated Press pre-season poll.

"That's absurd," Royal declared. "Just because that old ball's been rolling downhill doesn't mean it's going to keep going."

The downhill roll stopped in the season-opener. With Nebraska holding a 14-7 lead in the fourth quarter, Texas Quarterback Mike Cotten engineered a 73-yard touchdown march. The Longhorns then decided to go for two points and a victory instead of settling for a tie. Cotten kept the ball but was mobbed by four Cornhuskers, who thus carted off a 14-13 win.

(Photo by Robert Willner)
Bear Bryant and Royal each get a hand on the Bluebonnet Bowl trophy after their
Alabama and Texas teams played to a 3-3 tie in the 1960 postseason game at Houston.

That started what Royal considers his most challenging year as a coach.

"We won three and lost three of our first six games," he recalled. "Then we made a strong finish that I think still represents one of our finest accomplishments. We won our last four when they were all toss-up games, and we were playing people just as good as we were; that was a real tribute to our football team."

Texas finished the regular season with a 7-3 record, then played a 3-3 tie with Alabama in the Bluebonnet Bowl.

"I thought there was more danger of our dropping below a five-five record that year than we'd ever had before," said Royal. "As a coach, I've never been below that figure but I think I know how bad it would make me feel. I know, too, that success breeds success—so I've got to believe that failure breeds failure. I think our program would have been a long way towards hard times if that team hadn't rallied."

The rally started with a convincing 17-7 conquest of SMU in Austin. But it almost ran aground the next week in Waco, where Texas had to stave off a dangerous fourth-quarter passing attack to edge Baylor, 12-7. James Saxton, the skittery halfback who was to make All-America the following year, set up both Texas touchdowns; he took a pass from Cotten, good for 38 yards, to the Baylor 3 just as the first quarter ended, and he scooted 59 yards to the Baylor 12 early in the third quarter.

The Bears drove down to the Texas 29 during the last minute of play. Saxton knocked down a third-down pass and then, with only 22 seconds left to play, Tommy Lucas broke up a fourth-down screen pass.

Royal led the joyous delirium which resulted on the Texas bench, jumping into the air and clapping his hands as Cotten used up the remaining time by falling into the line.

In the locker room, before they let the sportswriters or anyone else come in, the happy Longhorns paused and said "The Lord's Prayer" together.

"One of the players suggested it—I don't recall which one," Royal explained later. "But we were all in a pretty thankful mood.

"I feel that the right to pray, and the time the players choose to pray, is very personal. If some of them want to have a prayer, they can have it—in the middle of practice, before a game, or after a game.

"I've always felt, though, that if you're going to say 'The Lord's Prayer,' you should say it just as quickly after a loss as after a victory. Praying before a game for a win, or giving thanks for a win after a game, really kinda bounces off the wall. I just believe the good Lord is occupied with more important things than football—and He's just as concerned with one side as He is the other. I don't think He's going to choose sides in the Texas-Baylor contest. I don't think that's what He controls and what He's sitting over."

Royal said his teams usually pray together three or four times a year and the pattern has not changed noticeably during recent years.

"On the basic things, I don't think kids have changed a heckuva lot from what they were even back when I was in school," he said. "Hair styles and dress codes have changed. But I look at Abe Lincoln and George Washington, at their pictures, and they look kinda funny to me. I didn't think so back there when I was in the first and second grades, coloring all those cherry trees and hatchets with Crayolas. I thought that was just the way George Washington was supposed to look. But trot him around there in about 1940 and he'd have looked kinda silly.

"I'm no longer disturbed over long hair or what youngsters wear. I'm more concerned about the basic things and I don't think those have changed."

He feels much the same way about religion and feels that the basics, not the "frills," are what count. And he has some strong religious beliefs.

Royal grew up as a Church of Christ member but began attending the Presbyterian Church when he went to Mississippi State.

"I never have really felt that it's a big deal whether you're a Baptist or Methodist or Episcopalian or Presbyterian or Catholic or whatever," he declared. "I don't think it matters whether you're totally immersed or sprinkled. Or whether you have a piano in the church or don't have a piano. Or whether you have communion every three months or every week.

"People sit around and argue about those things but I just can't see that they're important in living a Christian life. I've heard many a sermon saying that you're not baptized unless you're totally immersed, because that's what the Bible says. But that's a matter of interpretation, on what the Bible says. I think the thought behind baptism, the giving of yourself and dedicating yourself, is the thing that's important—not the ritual of how you go about it.

"Each denomination varies a little bit in those areas but they don't vary on the basics. To me, the basics are what's important: that there is a God, that Christ was here, Christ lived, Christ died, Christ arose, your sins can be forgiven, there's a place for us after this life—all these things are basics. All the other things are what I call the 'frills.'

"If you're running a gas station and a guy pays you for a gallon of gas, but you cut it short and don't give him all he's paying you for, I don't think there is any sort of ritual you can go through on Sunday morning that will make up for that. That's just not right. But if you treat people the way you want them to treat you, then I think you're on pretty safe ground regardless of the ritual you go through in church.

"I think doing right by your fellow man is important; that's basic. My ideas on Christian living come pretty much from the teachings of my Dad. These are things like not lying, not cheating, not being deceitful, paying your debts, doing what you tell people you're going to do and living up to what you say—even if you make an agreement that you find out later is going to hurt you. If you make an agreement with someone who accepts it in good faith, you should follow on through with it—unless circumstances change to the point that both parties agree to call it off."

This philosophy led Royal to stick with Tulsa, when Oklahoma offered him a job, even though he had not actually signed a contract at the time. And it prompted him to secure an amicable release from every contract he left en route to Texas. It also affected his feelings about prayer.

"Prayer is not meant to be just on Saturday afternoons and I don't think religion is something that ought to be used to try to win football games or inspire football players," he said. "That's why I've always been a little reluctant to pray *before* a game.

"If you're not careful, especially when kids are stirred up and emotional, you might inject prayer or religion at that time—and I don't think that's right, to get the adrenalin flowing and try to get an extra effort that way.

"I don't think religion ought to be excluded from anything but I want to be sure that I don't use it to stir people up emotionally to try to win a football game. I do think that religion gives you strength, determination, encouragement, and peace of mind—whether you're a football player or anything else."

Royal had to rely heavily on his deep religious faith in facing three tragic deaths during an 11-year period. Reggie Grob, a fourth-string sophomore guard, suffered a heat stroke on the first day of fall practice in 1962 and died after being in a coma for 18 days. Steinmark, a pint-sized safety man, helped Texas score its great 15-14 victory over Arkansas in the final regular season game of 1969, cinching the national championship; six days later, his left leg was amputated because of cancer and he died on June 6, 1971.

Then, in March of 1973, Royal's 27-year-old daughter, Mrs. Marian Kazen, and her two small children were injured when a bus smashed into her car on an Austin street. Marian was in a coma for 20 days before she died.

Among the first people the Royals heard from after Marian's accident were Warren and Thelma Grob, Reggie's parents. And that meant a lot, because the nightmare the Royals endured in 1973 turned out to be quite similar to that of the Grobs in 1962. In both cases, Royal spent much of his time at Austin's Brackenridge Hospital.

"I felt I knew what Thelma and Warren were going through when Reggie was in the hospital—but I really didn't, until it happened to me," Royal said later. "You have hope at first, and maybe see a little progress, and you're grasping at every straw; then you start seeing the gradual decline, until the last few days—when you realize there's not much chance and that, really, it's just a matter of time . . . ."

After specialists completed an extensive examination of Marian on

Sunday, April 8, Royal was told that there was no hope and that she probably would die within a few days. She died the following Wednesday.

Until this tragedy took place, Royal felt that about the worst things he had ever gone through were the deaths of Grob and Steinmark.

"You've got to second-guess yourself when something like Grob's death occurs," he said. "Should we have run wind sprints that day? If we'd just called off practice five minutes earlier, or if someone hadn't been quite as demanding—. All these things run through your head.

"But I don't recall anyone pushing Reggie. I think it was his own drive and his own competitiveness that made him go beyond the point where he should have dropped out.

"Now, we school 'em and instruct 'em and caution 'em that if they're ever woozy or feel they can't run, to drop out and not feel bad about it. We'll understand—we know it's hot and this is a safety thing. We tell 'em that if there is any doubt in their minds, to drop out. We hadn't done that before because we'd never experienced anything of that kind. And we really were not aware, until then, of how dangerous it was.

"We're constantly aware of the heat, especially during two-a-day practices. I'm always looking around for anybody that's kind of wobbly. We take breaks often and we let 'em drink all the water they want. I don't care how much water they drink during practice now; each individual knows how much he needs."

Royal remains deeply grateful for the friendship and understanding of Grob's parents.

"They could have blamed me, or ridiculed me or severely criticized me," he noted. "Parents love their children so much that sometimes it's impossible for them to be objective about something like this. Their minds just become locked. But that wasn't the case at all with Warren and Thelma. We had several communications from them when we lost Marian and they all had a special meaning."

Grob's death hit Royal so hard that he thought about getting out of coaching. And if he had decided to quit, he said, he would have done so immediately, without waiting until the end of that season.

"I'm not going to hang around after I decide to quit," he declared. "There were a few days when I felt like it just wasn't worth it. I was emotional and upset. I think it would have been a mistake, as far as my future happiness and everything . . . ."

Grob died on Tuesday before the season-opener with Oregon. The Longhorn team went to Houston by bus for his funeral on Friday and when someone asked Co-captain Pat Culpepper if the tragedy might affect Texas' play the next night, he declared: "We're all sorry this happened, but we won't have any excuses."

Texas defeated Oregon, 25-13. One of the most reassuring things about that game, to Royal, was the fact that Warren Grob attended it.

The Longhorns had to overcome a 3-13 disadvantage during the second half. They went ahead only after Tackle Jim Besselman, who also had suffered from heat exhaustion on the first day of practice, recovered a fumble on the Oregon 5-yard line.

Royal was not really thrilled over the Longhorns' performance, noting that they were lucky to be behind by only three points (6-3) at halftime. But when a few of the fans complained about the closeness of the final score, he expressed resentment.

"A few years ago, people around here were looking for a win of any kind," he said. "Now, they want to win *big.*"

(Photo by Bill Malone)
Darrell presents an autographed football from his 1963 national championship team to one of his biggest fans, former Governor Allan Shivers.

Chapter 12

THE CORONATION

A few days after Texas finished that fateful, dramatic 1962 season with a 13-3 victory over Texas A&M, Darrell and Edith Royal went to Acapulco with two of their closest friends, Mr. and Mrs. Jack Perry of Houston, for a four-day vacation.

They had plenty to celebrate. That 14-14 tie with Rice turned out to be the only blot on the Longhorns' record and Texas chalked up its first undefeated season since 1923. The Longhorns also won the Southwest Conference championship outright for the first time since 1952 (they had tied for it in 1953, 1959 and 1961) and the host role in the Cotton Bowl opposite LSU. And, at the start of that season, Royal had been named director of athletics with a salary raise to $20,000 a year.

The Royals and the Perrys were in a gala mood when they arrived in Acapulco—but they were hardly prepared for the earth-shaking experience which awaited them.

"I had just gotten a hair cut—more or less," Royal related later. "That barber was just gouging out big hunks of hair so I finally told him to stop. I'd had enough of that.

"Jack was getting a shave—also more or less. His barber seemed to be shaving off about half the whiskers and pulling out the others. I went outside to wait and was standing there watching some little Mexican boys pitch pennies.

"I was standing between two tall buildings. All of a sudden, I heard this big rumble. Those little boys' eyes all got as big as doughnuts and I realized we were having an earthquake.

"I took off down the middle of the street, trying to get to the plaza where nothing could fall on me. A big chunk of concrete and brick fell off about a three-story bulding, right at my feet. It didn't miss me more than a foot or so. And it was big enough that it would have given me considerably more than just a headache.

"The whole thing was over in about ten seconds, but it really was a close call. And I'll bet you I covered at least a hundred yards during those ten seconds. In fact, after it was over, some of the natives had some fun laughing about how fast I was on my feet."

Royal went back to the barber shop and found that Perry, a former

Longhorn baseball player, also had found speed he did not know he had. Perry had taken off with a barber's cloth hanging around his neck and his face half-covered with lather. He also returned to the barber shop, as did Edith and Mrs. Perry, who had been shopping.

"When we all got back there," said Royal, "the barber insisted that everything was okay and he wanted to finish shaving Jack's face. He was holding that razor—and his hand was shaking like a leaf. Jack said, 'No, thanks,' and we got out of there."

A month later, almost to the day, LSU really shook up Royal's world by drubbing the Longhorns, 13-0, in the Cotton Bowl.

When he arrived in Dallas for the game, Royal predicted "a real close one which could go either way." He also responded to criticism of his team's rather lack-luster offense by declaring: "We've had some people say, after we beat 'em, that we weren't so good. That reminds me of my little kid: after I give him a whipping, he goes in the back room and says it didn't hurt. I've never been kicked in the seat of the pants by anyone who was in front of me, I'll tell you that. I just want to keep all those people behind me and not let them get in front. They can kick all they want to from back there."

After the game, Royal readily admitted that the whipping administered by LSU hurt him—considerably.

"But, bitter as it is, it still has some value," he philosophized. "I don't believe you can appreciate success unless you've known defeat." However, he is convinced that it doesn't take much defeat to serve that purpose.

Royal once observed that football coaches are the hardest people in the world to please "because each one wants to have the best team in the country but doesn't want anyone else to know it until the end of the season."

Before the start of the 1963 season, there were strong suspicions in some quarters that Royal might have the best team in the nation. In the pre-season ratings, Texas was picked Number One by both *Sports Illustrated* and the *Street & Smith Football Yearbook*. The AP poll rated the Longhorns fifth.

Royal insisted then that everyone was overrating his team and that it was not as good as it had been the year before. He also figured that his first opponent was the heat; with Grob's death a year earlier still fresh on his mind, he kept a wary eye on both heat and humidity during early September workouts, cutting some of them short. And he received quite a scare when two of the Longhorns became woozy and went to the hospital, where they were kept three days as a precautionary measure before being released.

By the time Texas opened against Tulane in New Orleans, Royal was gloomy over a rash of injuries but felt good about the way Duke Carlisle had taken charge at quarterback.

The Longhorns rolled over Tulane (21-0), Texas Tech (49-7) and Oklahoma State (34-7), moving up to the Number Two spot in the weekly polls just before they played top-ranked Oklahoma. But the Oklahoma State victory was a costly one: Fullback Ernie Koy, a potential All-America and a great punter, suffered a shoulder separation early in that game.

The following Monday, doctors operated on Koy and put a metal screw in his shoulder, sidelining him for the rest of the season—and it was almost like driving a nail into Royal's heart.

When he picked Harold Philipp to replace Koy at fullback, Royal commented, "He doesn't have a whole lot of speed—but maybe Elizabeth Taylor can't sing."

Finding a replacement punter was a bit more difficult. Royal finally picked Kim Gaynor, a reserve wingback, and aroused a covey of criticism when he commented, "Old Ugly's better than Old Nothing." He had to explain later that he was not referring to Gaynor's appearance but was merely utilizing one of those old Hollis expressions, which originated when someone asked a young man why he had dated an unattractive girl.

Gaynor was not a long-distance kicker, averaging only 32.6 yards per punt that season. But, fortunately, good punting turned out to be far less essential than usual for that Texas team.

The Longhorns went into their "game of the century" with Oklahoma favored by five points. The usual sell-out of tickets made it possible for Dallas and Austin stations to televise the game—but only after fans contributed $9,091 to buy up all remaining tickets to a conflicting Trinity University game in San Antonio.

The Texas-OU game, pitting the nation's two top-ranked teams against each other, turned out to be far less exciting than anyone had expected. The Longhorns took charge early, with Carlisle tearing up the Sooner defense on the option play and with Tackle Scott Appleton wrecking its offense. Texas rang up a 21-0 lead before Oklahoma scored, late in the third quarter, and came away with a 28-7 victory which stands in Royal's mind as one of the most pleasing and memorable of his career.

A few days later, Texas moved up to Number One in the polls. Royal issued a grim reminder that this was the third consecutive year, and the fourth during the previous five, that the Longhorns had been top-rated—in midseason. And the honor had been quite temporary on all four of those occasions, he noted.

"You've got to feel good about being Number One," he admitted, "but I'm not blinded by it. You always want to finish Number One at the end of the season but I think any coach realizes that, on any given day, there are fifteen or twenty college football teams that could beat his."

He conceded that Texas probably would be favored in each of its six remaining games.

"If and when we get beat, it will be an upset," he declared. "We'll probably be favored in each individual game; but there's no way you can lump the six games we've got to play and figure we can win all of 'em."

Despite the pressure they can produce, Royal feels that the weekly polls are beneficial for football—primarily because they provide a tantalizing subject for conversation over coffee cups and stir up interest.

"But I really don't pay much attention to them until the end of the year," he said in a 1973 interview. "And then, after the end of the year, it's short because you've got to begin getting ready for next season. And where we ranked last year doesn't mean a tinker's dam when it comes to that. Sure, I like to be high in the polls—and I'm glad we finished third in the nation last year. But you could quiz me on some of those other years, except when we were first, and I couldn't even tell you where we finished.

"I do remember that, in 1958, the week before the Rice game, we were rated fourth in the nation and I knew we weren't that good. I called Bobby Dodd, because I'd always respected his ideas and his thoughts. I asked him, 'How do you handle a situation like this? We're not that good a football team and I just don't feel like we're ready to play.'

"There wasn't much Dodd could say except, 'You do have a problem.' He really wasn't able to help me any."

The problem became obvious to everyone when Rice slaughtered the Longhorns, 34-7. And the next Monday, Royal gave his squad a day off from practice, explaining that the players had been working hard and "you can get tired even of chocolate cake—a day of rest won't hurt them."

Five years after that 1958 debacle, Royal remembered it well as his Longhorns approached the Rice game, their sixth of the season. And the Owls gave the 1963 Texas team one of its many close shaves as it accomplished what Royal considered the impossible and went unde-feated.

Of those last six games Royal dreaded so much, only the one with TCU was relatively easy. Texas took a 17-0 decision in that one after beating Arkansas, 17-13; Rice, 10-6; SMU, 17-12; and Baylor, 7-0. But the toughest game of all, for a number of reasons—including some which had nothing to do with football—was the traditional season finale against Texas A&M.

Six days before that climactic clash, Royal went home at noon to change clothes before going to Bergstrom Air Force Base to help greet President John F. Kennedy. Royal was to be in the welcoming party when Kennedy arrived in Austin from Dallas on Nov. 22, 1963.

"I was getting dressed, and a TV set was on," Royal recalled. "They broke in on a soap opera to give a bulletin, saying the President had been shot. I was shocked, like everybody else, I guess. I just stopped dressing and sat there, waiting to get the details . . . ."

Royal said the Kennedy assassination had a far greater impact on the Longhorns than he thought it would have. The shock was compounded by the wounding of Gov. John Connally, a Texas ex and avid football fan who had visited in the locker room many times.

"I felt like we were all geared up and ready to go," said Royal. "We were sitting on an undefeated season. And then there was talk about the game being postponed, or maybe even called off. Everybody seemed to be in a sort of state of shock. No one felt like working out. We had all the momentum going, and everybody was eager and enthusiastic and aggressive, and then, poof! It was just like sticking a needle in a balloon. Everybody suddenly was deflated.

"We never did get pumped back up again—and some miraculous things had to happen in that A&M game for us to win it . . . ."

The game was to be televised nationally; that fact, ironically, contributed to the terrible condition of the playing field at College Station.

"It was a horribly muddy field," recalled Royal, who showed his displeasure before the game by using a rake to test the depth of the mud. "They'd worked out on that field, and made chugholes in it. Then they brought in fresh dirt to level it up—and they sprayed that with some green dye, so it would look pretty on television. I found out later that was the equivalent itself to an inch and a half rain. Then it rained on top of that, so it was nothing but goo.

"I don't think it was intentional, but it was a terrible mistake. And I didn't think anybody would score."

But Texas marched down to the Aggie 11 the first time it got the ball and Crosby kicked a 27-yard field goal.

Even then, Royal thought that would be all of the scoring. He turned to Coach Pittman and said, "Well, we've got ours."

Two touchdown passes thrown by Jim Keller gave the Aggies a 13-3 lead in the third quarter but then an Aggie fumble, at the A&M 35, enabled Texas to cut the deficit to four points. The Longhorns tried for a 2-point conversion and failed; that left them needing a touchdown to win.

With only five minutes left to play, Quarterback Tommy "The Rifleman" Wade came off the bench and passed the Longhorns from their own 20 to the A&M 2. He was blessed with some wonderful cooperation from the Aggies; once, an Aggie defender intercepted one of his passes but tried to lateral it and Texas recovered at the A&M 45.

There was only one minute and 19 seconds left to play when Carlisle dived over the goal line from one yard out, giving Texas a 15-13 victory.

In the locker room, Royal received a call from Mrs. Connally. She was at the Governor's bedside in a Dallas hospital and wanted to extend his congratulations.

"She said the Governor watched all of it on television that she would permit him to," Royal reported, "but she cut it off because he was getting too worked up. I told her that if I'd had a switch so I could have turned it off, I would have, too."

The day before the game, the Longhorn squad had sent a telegram to Connally saying:

"Tomorrow when we face the Aggies we will be confronted with the most important challenge of our athletic careers. You have given us added courage to face this challenge with the way you have met your adversity jaw to jaw. We are looking forward to your speedy recovery and the day you join us back in Austin."

After the A&M game, several Texas players admitted they had really been jolted by the assassination of President Kennedy.

"Most of the guys took it real hard," said Appleton, one of the captains. "We had to force it out of our minds. We knew we had to get out of the depressed state we were in . . . .

"He was everybody's president."

Texas seemed to be everybody's national champ—almost. After the regular season ended, Texas was handed that honor by the Associated Press, United Press International and the National Football Foundation, which voted to give its silver MacArthur Bowl trophy to the Longhorns.

After only ten years as a head coach in college football, Royal had achieved the dream of a lifetime—a national championship. Or had he? There was dissent from partisans of Navy, which had lost only one game (to SMU, 32-38) and would face Texas in the Cotton Bowl. The taunts from Annapolis proved a blessing in disguise to Texas.

"I felt it was unfair," Royal said later, "for Navy, which lost to SMU—which we had defeated—to come in there and say that if they beat Texas, they'd be the national champs. The last game shouldn't count any more than a loss in the middle of the season, if you're judging it on the whole season.

"I really didn't have to say much to our players," he added, with a grin. "Navy was taking care of everything I had to say."

In view of the suddenly mushrooming demands on Royal's personal appearance schedule, this was most fortunate. Showered with honors and invitations, he returned to Austin on Dec. 16 to put his squad back to work after a two-week layoff. At that point, he was bouncing around like a yo-yo.

"I've just spent successive nights in New York, Bay City, New York, Denver and Dallas," he said, as he prepared to leave for a high school football banquet in Angleton.

If there is such a thing as being disappointed at a banquet at which you are presented the national championship trophy, Royal was—at the National Football Foundation affair. The former army staff sergeant sat next to General Douglas MacArthur at the head table and was anxious to hear him discuss some of his famous military exploits.

"But the General was like everyone else," said Royal, who has an insatiable curiosity about all sorts of things. "All he wanted to do was talk about football and ask me questions about it."

Meanwhile, Navy's taunts about the national championship went on right up until the Cotton Bowl kickoff. During the pregame introductions

Royal, General Douglas MacArthur and Wales Madden, then a member of the UT Board of Regents, celebrated the awarding of the MacArthur Bowl, symbolic of the national championship, to Texas on December 11, 1963, in New York.

on national television, Navy Coach Wayne Hardin declared: "When the challenger meets the champion and the challenger wins, then there's a new champion "

Royal was introduced a few moments later and declared, "We're ready!"

They were. The game was only three minutes old when Carlisle lofted a 58-yard touchdown pass to Phil Harris. Then, in the second quarter, the team that had a reputation for disdaining the forward pass used it again—this time on a 63-yard touchdown strike from Carlisle to Harris.

Texas wound up with a 28-6 victory which made even Hardin admit, "I've never seen a team which deserved to be Number One more than Texas."

The undisputed title of "Number One" turned out to be a mixed blessing for Royal, but it was one he could find no fault with at the time. In three years, he had won 30 games, lost only two and tied one. The Football Writers Association and the Helms Foundation, having waited until after the bowl games, joined the chorus and hailed Texas as the National Champion. The American Football Coaches Association named Royal "Coach of the Year" and the Texas Sports Writers Association once again picked him as "Southwesterner of the Year."

Amid the accolades was one which probably meant more than all the others put together, and which would blossom into a friendship destined to play a major role in Royal's life. It came from President Lyndon B. Johnson.

Royal accepted an invitation to address the Texas State Society in Washington on March 1, 1964. The Royals flew to Washington with several of their friends, including the Perrys and Mr. and Mrs. Frank Denius of Austin.

They had met the Johnsons earlier, at a Headliners Club function in Austin. But Royal was quite surprised when he saw President Johnson in Washington and was invited to come by the White House that afternoon for a visit. That was a far cry from the time he hitch-hiked to Childress in 1936 to see President Roosevelt. But he did not realize what a "far cry" it really was until he went to the White House and received treatment normally accorded only to members of the President's family and his close personal friends.

"He showed us through their living quarters and spent a lot of time with us," said Royal. "In fact, I was amazed that he had that much time to spend with us. And, even more amazing, he invited us to come back the next day. He had a dinner engagement that night, at Pierre Salinger's, but when he left he told us to stay and look around all we wanted to. And he told the guards to let us do whatever we wanted to do.

"This is kinda worn out, I guess, and sounds trite, but this was a personal experience that was very meaningful to me. And this country is about the only place where it could happen—where you're picking fruit, and trying to find some way to make enough money to eat on, and then, in a few years, you're visiting with the President of the United States—not just in the White House but in his living quarters there. That's quite a contrast.

"President Johnson had to know how inquisitive we were about the presidency—and also how nervous we were. He took a coupla phone calls up there while we were with him and I tried not to pay any attention, because I knew it wasn't any of my business . . . ."

Royal's business was strictly college football and he was being acclaimed almost universally as the best in the business, a king of the sport. About the only exception was the Washington Touchdown Club, which drew all sorts of ridicule when it honored Navy as its "National Champion" and Navy Coach Hardin as "Coach of the Year."

When Royal began his speech to a combined meeting of the Texas State Society and the UT Ex-Students Club of Washington, a photographer shot several pictures of him.

"If you catch me smiling," Royal quipped, "send it to the Washington Touchdown Club."

Chapter 13

A SATCHEL FULL OF MONEY

It took some time for Royal to realize that success *can* breed
failure—when the joys of a championship season, with all the resultant
speaking invitations, take you away from the long, sometimes "degrading" but highly necessary process of recruiting football players.

Royal admits that he made so many personal appearances during the
early part of 1964, in the wake of that first national championship, that
he spent far less time on recruiting than he should have. It seems both
ironical and logical that he personally was the target of some determined
recruiting efforts at that time.

Wilkinson resigned from Oklahoma after the 1963 season and made
an unsuccessful bid, in 1964, for the Republican nomination to the U.S.
Senate. Almost before Wilkinson's resignation hit the table, a great many
Oklahoma fans began clamoring for Royal; in addition, many of his old
teammates phoned him and tried to talk him into "coming home."

Royal told everyone, from the start, that he was not interested in the
Oklahoma job. Some found that hard to believe, especially in view of the
fact that he had held eight jobs in eight years before Texas hired him.
Royal admitted that he had a reputation in 1957 for being "unstable" but
said every move he made was a progressive one, from the standpoint of his
career.

"I was searching for something," he explained once, "and I found it
at Texas . . . ."

Strangely enough, he had an especially strong feeling *against*
returning to OU.

"I didn't want to follow Bud," Royal declared many years later.
"He'd have been a hard act to follow. And people up there would
remember me as a student. Down here, the only way they've ever thought
of me is as 'coach.' If I go back up there, then I'm rubbing elbows and
working with people who knew me when I was in school.

"Later on, it wouldn't have made that much difference but at that
time, I thought it made *quite* a difference. And I really didn't think there
was any better chance to succeed there than at Texas. I like
money—anybody likes money; but I've decided that money is not a real
big factor in my happiness. And I knew I was happy here.

"I know I love living in the State of Texas. I still have good friends in Oklahoma, and I love my friends up there, but I'd rather live in Austin, Texas. For one thing, I've got more people that I know in Austin—

"Look, in Oklahoma, I lived in a little ol' town of three thousand people. Then I was a student at the University of Oklahoma for four years. That's not like living and working down here for ten or twelve years. Hands down, I know more people in Texas than I know in Oklahoma. *This* is home, now.

"Oklahoma kinda had to contact me, to satisfy some of the people up there. They had to get me to turn down the job, publicly, so they could hire a coach. They didn't think I was going to come but they really had to force me to say I was going to stay at Texas. Then they could say they'd tried to hire me, and they could go hire a coach."

More recently, Royal has been contacted by several professional football teams who, in effect, asked him to just name his price.

"I don't want to go to some place like Boston and start a new life, at my age," he declared. "I don't have that many bullets left. Wouldn't I be miserable if I went some place like that and had a satchel full of money but wasn't happy? I couldn't think of anything worse.

"I've got enough to pay my bills and get by comfortably, and I'm doing all right. I'm not making a bunch of money but I'm happy, and what else is there? Why should I take some other job when it couldn't make me any happier?"

Royal noted that his position permits him to "do a lot of things and go a lot of places just like I was rich."

As an example, he noted that he vacations every year in Cuernavaca, Mexico, as a guest of Johnny Thompson, a Texas ex who is chairman of the Board of the Southland Corporation. It was after the 1959 season that the Royals first visited Cuernavaca—at that time with Joe C. Thompson, Johnny's father, who was then a member of the UT Board of Regents and has since died.

"That was one of the most pleasurable two or three days I'd ever experienced," Royal recalled. "Coming back, Mr. Thompson said he'd like to visit with me so our wives sat together on the plane and we sat together."

During the flight, Thompson asked Royal if he would be willing to sign a long-term contract with the University of Texas.

"Certainly," said Royal. "That's something any coach would like—because this is kind of a shaky profession we're in."

"Well, how would you feel about your obligation to fulfill it?" Thompson asked.

"How long a contract are you talking about?" asked Royal.

"Ten years."

Royal thought a moment and then replied: "If the University of Texas Regents had that much confidence in me, to obligate themselves and tie themselves down to ten years, I'd feel obligated to fulfill the contract."

Nothing was mentioned about salary—and Royal takes some pride in the fact that he never has asked for a raise in pay. Thompson initiated the ten-year contract, at the same $17,500 a year Royal was making, and Royal signed it. His first raise came after the 1962 season, boosting him to $20,000. Early in 1964, after winning the national championship, he was raised to $24,000 and given a full professorship, with tenure—which he figured was more important than the money.

In fact, the security offered by that tenure provision caused Royal to lose track of how long his contract had to run.

"It really doesn't matter," he explained. "If a substantial number of people—responsible people—don't want me to coach football any more, I have a commitment that I'll be on the faculty. So if the people in authority want me to quit coaching, I'll quit. I really don't know whether I've got three years left on my contract or eight years, but I don't care. They can make it day to day, if they want to."

Royal's annual salary was raised to $30,000 on Jan. 1, 1966, to $35,000 on Sept. 1, 1969, and to $40,000 on Jan. 1, 1972. His fringe benefits include a substantial amount of money from his weekly television program during the football season and from some endorsements.

When Oklahoma made its first overtures to Royal in 1964, the elder Thompson had died of cancer. Royal did not know if he had ever told anyone of their conversation on that plane flying back from Mexico, when the young coach agreed to stay at Texas for ten more years.

Royal called Johnny Thompson and asked if his father had ever told him about the agreement. The younger Thompson said he had not, so Royal related the conversation to him.

"I just wanted you to know that I promised your dad I wouldn't be hopping this contract, and I'm not going to," said Royal, "regardless of what you might be hearing from Oklahoma during the next few days. I want you to know that this thing is going to take another day or so, before it's made clear in the newspapers, but I told your dad I was staying at Texas—and I'm going to."

No one ever mentioned the agreement to Royal, leading him to believe that the elder Thompson had never told anyone about it. But it was one which Royal felt obligated to keep, even if he never received a salary raise. And he found it was one that was fairly easy to keep, even in the face of highly lucrative offers from the pros.

"I don't want a big ol' house and a lot of those things," said Royal. "I've never learned to live real fast and real luxuriously, anyway, so I thought about those offers and it still came back to the same answer: I don't want to fool around with happiness.

"If somebody was giving me a hard time, or I couldn't get along with the people I have to work under and I hadn't been accepted, and if I was getting a little guff or something, I might look at it differently. But, fortunately, I haven't had that situation.

"Oh, if I didn't have the support I need or had some people here who wanted me to leave, I could go somewhere else and start over. But I've had about as unanimous backing as I could have.

"Money doesn't tempt me," he declared. Then, thoughtfully, he added, "Of course, if I was broke, it would."

With Royal's background, it is easy for him to understand how young high school football stars can be tempted by money and lured to colleges by illegal financial aid. But when a close friend asked him, after he had won his third national championship in 1970, why Texas did not "cheat" in recruiting, he replied: "I think we could, and get away with it. But I've never done it and I'm not going to start now. As a matter of fact, I'm going to start turning in everybody I find cheating—or else get out of coaching."

Royal has since waged a relentless war against illegal recruiting. The University of Texas has taken the lead in urging major colleges and universities to finance an all-out war against subsidization of athletes.

"I think everybody's concerned about this," said Royal. "They're going to have to crack down. The involvement of alumni is the big thing. If the alumni stayed completely out of it, you could police it one thousand percent better."

Royal recognizes recruiting as the lifeblood of coaching and traces his greatest success to two great recruiting years—1958, when he brought in the Saxton-Collins crowd, and 1967, when Texas rounded up the "Steve Worster bunch."

"There were a lot of good football players in that Worster crowd," said Royal. "They started playing for us as sophomores and we've recruited pretty good ever since—not super, but pretty good.

"There's nothing funny about recruiting," he added. "And the thing that's irritating is that some of the people who are being recruited think it *is* funny. They think it's a ball, and a blast, and a lot of fun, and party time. They think it's kind of funny how coaches compete, and wait around for their turn. I don't think it's very funny, myself. In a sense, it's degrading. And it's getting worse."

Although Royal detests underhanded tactics in recruiting, his pet peeve is something much more common, more innocent and more obvious. It is the blaring of a television set which competes with conversation. He also dislikes conversation when it competes with television, or live entertainment—or even golf.

While he authored the statement that you can get too much of anything, even chocolate cake, he never has extended that reasoning to golf. During the off season, he figures 36 or 45 holes of golf as a pretty fair day's recreation. And once, he recalled, he and Arkansas Coach Frank Broyles "got in eighty holes one day, up at Fayetteville."

"We get right at it," Royal explained, "when we get going. We don't pitch a lot of grass and line up a lot of putts. You can't talk about a lot of other things and play golf, either. If I wanted to do that, I'd rather go sit down somewhere and talk.

"And when I go sit down and try to talk to someone, I don't like to have a television set going. That irritates me as much as anything, when I'm recruiting. I go in to see people and they've got the television set blaring, loud. They leave it going while you're sitting there, trying to make your pitch. When people come to see me, if we're visiting, I've gotta turn that television off. Of course, if there's something on that everybody wants to see, then we all turn and watch TV and do our visiting later.

"I feel the same way about any entertainment—and how sorry the entertainment is, or how good, doesn't matter," said Royal, who has been known to ask other patrons in night clubs to quiet down during floor shows.

In his own home, where some of the greatest of the country-western musicians have performed, he will not tolerate even the most discreet whispering while they're "pickin'" and singing. He and Edith have stayed up all night, at times, listening to such stars—with Royal insisting that all the guests be quiet during the performances.

"If you don't want entertainment, you don't have to go to a place where they have it," he reasons. "If you want to drink and talk, there are plenty of saloons; you can go find one of those. I can't understand why people will go to a place where they know there's entertainment, then sit there and talk louder than the entertainment.

"And it really irritates me if they're trying to talk to me. But it's also irritating if they're over at another table, just interfering with my listening and the listening of other people. That's about as rude as you can be, really. If a guy doesn't like the entertainment, he can get up and walk out. That's fine. But he ought to let the other people have the chance to stay there and listen—and he ought to let the entertainer have a chance."

Royal's natural inclination is to concentrate completely on anything he does—whether it be shining shoes, throwing newspapers, playing football, coaching football, playing golf, listening to music or recruiting. He doesn't like for anything to interfere and, in 1964, a lot of things—notably speaking engagements and coaching clinic appearances —interfered with his recruiting.

But the 1964 season itself was a great one. Texas bashed everyone around pretty good, with the exception of Arkansas, to compile a 9-1 regular season record. When Royal complained at the start of that season about not having an experienced quarterback, Broyles commented: "With the backfield he's got, Darrell could get a *student* to hand the ball off to them."

Marvin Kristynik turned out to be a student who could hand the ball off reasonably well—and even throw it, when necessary.

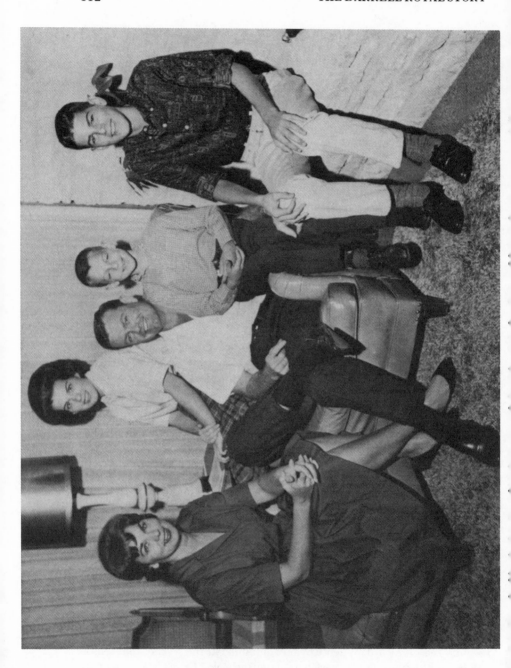

Texas went into the Arkansas game, its fifth of the season, ranked Number One in the nation. But Ken Hatfield returned a punt 81 yards for an Arkansas touchdown in the second quarter and Texas did not catch up until early in the fourth quarter, when a 2-yard plunge by Phil Harris capped a 46-yard drive.

Arkansas broke the 7-7 tie with a 34-yard touchdown pass from Fred Marshall to Bobby Crockett midway of the fourth quarter, taking a 14-7 lead. Texas took the subsequent kickoff and launched an exciting 70-yard, 16-play drive which was climaxed by Ernie Koy's one-yard touchdown blast with only one minute and 27 seconds left on the clock.

Now Royal, who had been tagged the "Barry Goldwater of college football" because of his conservatism, faced a crucial decision: should he try for two points and a victory, or settle for an extra point kick and a tie?

The champ should go down fighting if he goes down at all, without trying for a tie, Royal decided. He called a pass play and Kristynik's throw to Hix Green fell short.

"There was never any doubt in my mind about what to do," Royal said later, "That's one I'll never second-guess."

But it left Arkansas with a 14-13 victory, enabling the Razorbacks to finish the season undefeated and untied. That ended a 15-game winning streak for Texas and, for the first time since 1960, the Longhorns did not figure in the Southwest Conference championship picture. But the consolation prize for a 9-1 season wasn't too bad: a trip to the Orange Bowl to play Alabama, which was claiming the 1964 national championship.

When Alabama's great Joe Namath injured a knee in practice the week before the Orange Bowl Game, the margin by which the Crimson Tide was favored dropped from six points to three.

Koy broke the game open with a 79-yard touchdown sprint at the end of the first quarter. Six minutes later, the Longhorns shocked Alabama, a crowd of 72,000 in the Orange Bowl that New Year's night, and a nationwide television audience with a 69-yard scoring pass from Jim Hudson to Sauer. That stretched the Texas lead to 14-0.

But then Namath came out pitching, although Bryant said later he had not intended to play him. Namath completed six of his first 10 passes for 81 yards on an 87-yard scoring drive but Texas, after a long touchdown drive of its own, held a 21-7 lead at halftime.

Namath's passing produced another touchdown and a field goal for Alabama during the second half but Texas hung on for a 21-17 victory. Namath set a new Orange Bowl passing record, completing 18 of 37 for 255 yards. He won the game's most valuable player trophy but lost a crucial debate six minutes before the final gun, when the officials ruled that he had failed to crack the Texas goal line on a dramatic fourth-down plunge from the Texas one.

Bryant was magnanimous in his praise of both Namath and Royal.

"Coach Royal did a good job in preparation for this game—a better job than I did," said the 'Bama coach. "And I thought Namath's performance was the most courageous by any player I've ever seen."

He refused to quibble over that near miss at the Longhorn goal line.

"When you can't score from the one," said Bryant, "you don't deserve to win. Let's face it: Texas was just better prepared for this game than we were."

To Royal, that was indeed a high compliment, especially since he believes that "good luck" is what results when "preparation meets opportunity." But he looked back later and realized that he was not making adequate preparations at that time for the opportunities to be offered during the next few years.

"We didn't recruit well after the 1963 season," he reflected, "but we didn't run out of material until after '65."

Several times during those early championship seasons, Royal had warned that the Longhorns' good fortune couldn't last forever—especially when they were winning many of their games by paper-thin margins. And they were getting some lucky bounces which could not be attributed to preparation, or to anything else a coach could control.

"When we start losing—and our time's coming—I hope people will realize that I'm the same Darrell Royal," he said, "and that we're coaching the same way and doing the same things that have brought us success in the past.

"I'm not going to change but our luck's *bound* to change. We can't keep on getting all the good bounces. Those things have a way of evening up . . . ."

Chapter 14

DARK DAYS

The 1965 season opened on a bizarre, disaster-induced note which turned out to be most appropriate. Two days before the Longhorns were to play Tulane in New Orleans, the havoc wrought by Hurricane Betsy forced officials to switch the site to Austin. No one suspected at the time that the game would usher in what Royal considers his most disappointing year—and the first of three straight in which Texas posted 6-4 records for the regular season.

While 6-4 may be a goal at some schools, it is hardly acceptable by Royal's standards. And almost anyone who might have thought he was starting such a downhill slide in 1965 probably would have given 100-to-1 odds against his being able to maintain his sense of humor throughout it. But he did.

Seven Tulane fumbles helped Texas rack up a 31-0 victory in that transplanted season-opener. But the Longhorns failed to capitalize on several golden opportunities and after seeing the movies, Royal declared: "A large portion of it looked like recess football. When I was in grade school, we used to play football at recess. It would be just a bunch of pushing and grabbing. When it was time to go in, our teacher would wave a handkerchief. We should have waved a handkerchief out there Saturday night instead of blowing a whistle.

"We had too many people out there just playing around the edges," he added. "They'd get right up by it but then wouldn't participate full speed. That was disappointing. We've got too many boys that don't want to 'zap' the other side; they don't want to bust somebody, to really intimidate them."

He felt that was partly due to an unusually heavy rash of injuries which had plagued early September practice—and which was to be a continuing problem throughout the fall.

"The 1965 season was the most disappointing we've had," Royal declared many years later, "because we went six-four and our material really didn't call for us to be six-four. We were kinda fat and out of shape, then we got a bunch of injuries—and then our morale fell apart. We lost that heart-breaking game in Fayetteville, and then we lost to Rice in the poorest-played game since I've been at Texas—or anywhere else . . . ."

After the Longhorns swamped Texas Tech, 33-7, in their second game, they moved up to Number One in the AP poll and Number Two in the UPI poll.

Then a mediocre performance netted a 27-12 victory over Indiana, leaving Royal with complaints about his team's lack of consistency.

"As soon as we got a little money in our pockets," he declared after that one, "we walked off the job until we were broke again."

Texas disposed of Oklahoma, 19-0, the same day Arkansas whipped Baylor, 38-7, for its sixteenth consecutive victory. The Longhorns were ranked first in the nation and the Razorbacks third when they clashed in their nationally-televised "game of the century" the next Saturday in Fayetteville.

Football fever raged throughout Arkansas. The sea of red and the high-pitched partisanship which greeted the Longhorns in Fayetteville prompted Coach Campbell to observe, "This is like parachuting into Russia."

It proved to be just about that exciting. Even the preliminaries were packed with drama.

For instance, Jack Perry broke that speed record he had established during the Acapulco earthquake after Asst. Coach Charley Shira told him, as the Longhorns began dressing for the game, that Kristynik had lost his contact lenses. Shira said the quarterback suspected he had left them in the Fort Smith motel in which the Longhorns had spent the night.

Perry rushed out to the airport, flew his private jet to Fort Smith, found the lenses and, with the aid of a police escort, delivered them to Kristynik 15 minutes before game time.

A Longhorn fumble near their own goal line, another which landed in the hands of Arkansas' Tommy Trantham to start him on a 77-yard touchdown run, and a scoring pass from Jon Brittenum to Bobby Crockett gave the Porkers a 20-0 lead early in the second quarter.

Texas whittled the margin down to 20-11 before halftime and, thanks to the place-kicking of David Conway, came from behind to take a 21-20 lead in the third quarter.

With only four minutes left in the fourth quarter, Conway kicked his third field goal of the afternoon, a 34-yarder, and stretched the Longhorn lead to 24-20.

But Brittenum was far from through. He immediately launched an 80-yard drive, chewing Texas up with his passing. He finally slammed over for the last foot on a quarterback sneak with 1:32 left on the clock, giving Arkansas a 27-20 victory.

As hard as that one was for Royal to take, it was the next week that the roof really caved in on him. Texas, a 24-point favorite, ran up a 17-3 lead over Rice before the Owls came back to tie it up and then score a 20-17 win on Richard Parker's 33-yard field goal. Parker's dramatic kick beat the final gun by only 48 seconds.

"That has to be the sorriest game we've ever played," Royal remarked in 1973. "But Rice just doesn't play us like they play other people. In fact, I've always said that if alumni at other schools are unhappy with their teams, they should just come and watch them play Texas."

Ironically, especially in view of his 1962 experience against the Owls, Royal "second-guessed" himself on one of the plays he sent in from the bench. On the first play of the fourth quarter, with fourth down and one from the Rice 38, he sent Kristynik around left end. Kristynik lost a yard and Rice took over, starting a 61-yard drive for the touchdown which tied the score at 17-all.

"I wish now we had kicked, but that's hindsight," Royal declared. "I wasn't trying to win by two touchdowns when I took that chance; I was just trying to win by one point."

It was the first time since 1960 that Texas had lost two games in a row. And bizarre incidents continued to haunt the Longhorns. Early in the SMU game the next week, for instance, Conway tried a 43-yard field goal which hit the crossbar and bounced back. That turned out to be only the opening of a major disaster, a 31-14 SMU victory.

"I'm not going to panic and start changing our defense, or our offense, because we've lost three games," Royal said at his weekly press conference the next Monday.

"My confidence isn't shaken about our methods of doing things. We're going to stick with what we've been doing. There's an old saying, 'You dance with who brung you.' We'll keep doing the same things that have worked so well for us through the years and brought us to where we are. We're gonna dance with who brung us.

"If anything," he added, "we're going to get even more basic."

In looking at the statistics for that year, some people might suspect that Royal's basic philosophy about the forward pass had changed. The Longhorns completed 97 passes in 224 attempts during 1965 for 1,333 yards. The highest number of attempts by a Royal-coached team at Texas prior to that was in 1964, when Texas completed 63 of 151 for 900 yards.

The figures attracted an unusual amount of attention due to the growing legends about Royal's antipathy toward the forward pass. Those legends started, he insists, almost in jest when he made the oft-quoted statement that "Three things can happen to you when you pass—and two of 'em are bad."

"I was kinda razzing some of the writers when I said that," says Royal, "and it was really tongue-in-cheek. It was picked up that way at the time but it's been used so many times since that it sounds now like I had fire in my eyes when I said it.

"And I must admit that I've played the role a little bit. I kinda 'pooh-pooh' passing, but I really don't feel that way. I'm not 'anti-throw' at all, not a bit."

The record bears him out, especially when you look beyond the bare statistics. Royal's teams usually pass just as much as they need to in order to win—although he does believe that a good, solid running attack is a better investment than an aerial-oriented offense. As he has demonstrated in several highly dramatic situations, he will play a long shot when he thinks it necessary. And his anti-passing reputation has helped him surprise a few teams which were lulled into a false sense of security by it.

He also is inclined, at times, to fight fire with fire—such as in 1965, when Texas came out passing against Baylor's aerial circus. Kristynik threw three passes in the first quarter and all three went for touchdowns as Texas claimed a 35-14 victory.

But the next week provoked a brief discourse from Royal on locusts.

Four fumbles and a pass interception enabled TCU to score 22 points by moving the ball a total of only 105 yards as it upset the Longhorns, 25-10.

"These things happen to you when you're not playing well," said Royal. "I said when we were winning that these things usually even out—but durned if I don't think it's about even now.

"When the locusts arrive, they devour everything. When it rains, it pours. I wasn't blinded by the success we've had in the past because I knew that the difference between victory and defeat is so narrow— sometimes just a few inches.

"Overall, during my coaching career, I feel I've been blessed. More good things have happened to me than bad things. But right now, I have to look at that overall picture to keep from slitting my throat!"

Asked if he had conceived, before the season started, that he might lose four games out of his first nine, Royal replied: "I *always* conceive it—but nobody listens to me."

Just before the season finale with A&M, two more strange incidents seemed to put the crowning blow on that bewildering season. It was discovered that the first-down chain used in several Longhorn games was four inches longer than the prescribed 10 yards—a fact which came to light after a couple of engineers noticed it from the grandstand. But even that did not climax the bizarre circumstances of the '65 season.

Earlier that fall, Pittman had asked Royal who would replace Conway as the kicking specialist if they should lose him.

"How could we lose him?" asked Royal, noting that Conway would do nothing but kick. "Impacted wisdom tooth or something?"

One week before the A&M game, "something" offered a definite threat in that direction. Conway pulled a hamstring muscle in his leg—while running wind sprints in a physical education class.

"What else can happen to us?" asked Royal, when told that Conway might not be able to play against the Aggies. Had anyone been able to come up with the answer to that question, he would not have believed it.

The Aggies, facing second down and nine from their own 8-yard line early in the second quarter, brought in Jim Kauffman from the bench and deployed him as a wide flanker on the left side, for what they had dubbed their "Texas Special."

Quarterback Harry Ledbetter took the snap and threw what appeared to be an incomplete forward pass to Kauffman. The ball bounced in front of him and Kauffman picked it up, then kicked the ground in disgust as the Aggie linemen began going back for another huddle. End Dude McLean had gone down on a deep pass pattern. He paused—for only an instant, as the Texas defenders relaxed, not realizing the throw to Kauffman had been a *lateral*.

Then Kauffman lofted a long pass to McLean for 91 yards and a touchdown which set a new Southwest Conference record. But Royal had become accustomed to being on the wrong end of "new records" that year.

Still, the fates were not through toying with him. Conway did play against A&M—and committed a second-quarter error which led to an Aggie field goal. On fourth down and eight from the Texas 49, Conway was back to punt but juggled the ball and then tried to run around left end.

"I had plenty of time to kick when I first got the ball," he admitted later, "but for some reason I couldn't seem to get it turned right in my hands. I juggled it and then the rushers were on me, so I couldn't kick. I had to run and I would have made the first down but I pulled that muscle again when I started running."

That miscue contributed to the 17-0 lead which the Aggies held at halftime.

Royal spent only a few minutes in the locker room during the intermission. Standing in front of a blackboard, he diagrammed one minor change in pass defense strategy. Then he erased the lines he had drawn.

"I could stand up here and draw all kinds of diagrams," he declared, "but that wouldn't help us at this stage. It's too late now for diagrams. It's just a case now of how bad you want to win."

He turned and wrote on the blackboard, "21-17."

"That's what you *can* do," he declared. Then he turned and walked out of the dressing room, leaving the Longhorns a few more minutes to digest his words.

They took them to heart. They cut A&M's margin to 17-6 during the third quarter, then exploded for 15 points in the fourth. With All-America Linebacker Tommy Nobis leading a tremendous defensive effort, the Longhorns salvaged a 21-17 victory.

Although that was small consolation for that dismal season, Royal still managed to find a silver lining.

"It's going to be hard now for those other people to tell the high school prospects that if they go to Texas, they'll sit on the bench because we've got so much talent," he declared. "I think it's obvious that we have a lack of depth. We've had some good athletes in the past who could have helped us a lot, but who actually were afraid to come to Texas—they were afraid they wouldn't get to play here."

The University of Oklahoma made another ill-fated run at Royal in December of 1965, after chasing off Gomer Jones in the wake of a 3-7 season. Royal turned down a rumored $32,000 contract, with fringe benefits that would have boosted the figure to $50,000. That's when the University of Texas raised his salary from $24,000 a year to $30,000.

Royal decided to change his offense from the Wing T to the I formation and utilize a split end during the 1966 season. He poked fun at his anti-passing image in announcing this, saying: "Nobody believes me when I say we're going to use a split end. They're still talking about us not passing. Well, we passed more last year than we ever had before—and I guess they noticed that we also had our most disastrous season."

Despite the recent unpleasantness, Texas fans expected great things in 1966—especially from "Super Bill" Bradley, the phenomenal high school quarterback from Palestine. Bradley's publicity grew to such proportions that Royal expressed the fear that people would be coming to the stadium "expecting to see a water-walking act."

"The main thing I'm afraid of," he told Texas sportswriters during their tour of the fall training camps, "is that Bill will get to the point where he thinks he's got to deliver, and deliver big, on every play."

Bradley injured a knee during a 35-0 romp over Indiana, in the third game of the 1966 season, and never quite seemed to live up to his advance billing. But even Superman himself would have had trouble living up to that billing; as a matter of fact, Jones Ramsey used to confide to sportswriters that, in real life, "Super Bill" was "only Clark Kent."

Chris Gilbert was beginning to blossom but even he could not save Texas from a second straight 6-4 season. Nothing seemed to go right, as Royal recalls it.

"I remember that, in the SMU game, we were leading, twelve to ten, and had third down and one on the SMU thirty-three with about three minutes to play," said Royal. "I sent in a quarterback sneak, which I figure is about the safest play you can call. But we fumbled it and they recovered. Bradley made enough for a first down—but didn't have the ball. So then they kicked a thirty-two yard field goal, with about eighteen seconds left to play. They win, thirteen to twelve, and knock us out of a conference championship. So you've got to figure that luck is always a key element."

Luck certainly was a key element in the Longhorns' postseason appearance that year, which turned out to be a pivotal factor in recruiting.

"When we beat Ole Miss in the Bluebonnet Bowl, I felt like that stirred everyone up and renewed interest that had been kind of dormant for a while. We'd been wrestling around with those six-four years and still

Several of the people who played key roles in Royal's career joined him at the White House in January, 1966, when he presented a "Sportsman Award" to President Lyndon B. Johnson on behalf of the National Football Coaches Association. Left to right, Bud Wilkinson, Royal, Jake Gaither, President Johnson, Bear Bryant, Tonto Coleman and Duffy Daugherty.

had one more, 1967, in store. But I think we started the ball rolling at that time. That Ole Miss win was a big shot in the arm for us. If we were on the verge of disaster, that was it—and it was a delicate balance. But that started our finest recruiting year at Texas."

Royal said he was most reluctant, at first, to take a 6-4 team to the Bluebonnet Bowl.

"We went because Arkansas declined the invitation," he said. "Arkansas was invited first, but they'd just been beaten by Texas Tech and they declined.

"So Lou Hassel of the Bluebonnet Bowl called me, all out of breath, on Sunday morning and said they really needed help. I told him I didn't want to go. He asked me not to say 'no' but to think it over and let him call me back. I told him that would be fine and I'd think about it.

"I knew the Arkansas players had declined just because they were dejected and I urged the Bluebonnet Bowl to make another try at them. I didn't think we had a good enough team to go to a bowl. But I talked to our players and they wanted to go, so then I talked to the administration and the regents and everyone approved the idea. So when Hassel called back, I told him we'd come.

"Then, later that night, he called me back again and said Arkansas had changed its mind. They'd gone back home and decided they wanted to play in the Bluebonnet Bowl, after all.

"I said, 'Wait a minute; I've already talked to our players and the administration and everyone else. You tell me you want me to get the ox out of the ditch for you and, now that I've done it, you're telling me you want me to withdraw. After I've talked our boys into coming down there and playing, you're asking us to step aside so Arkansas can come.'

"He said, 'Well, if that's the way you feel about it, come on.'

"I told him that's exactly the way I felt about it at that point, although that morning I had tried to get him to talk Arkansas into coming."

Royal's original reluctance had been based partly, of course, on memories of that Jan. 1, 1958, fiasco with Ole Miss in the Sugar Bowl.

"But Lou said they really needed us, and I got to thinking that it might not be too bad and we might salvage something out of this ol' season," said Royal. "And we really did. It turned out to be one of the best things that could possibly have happened to us. There was a lot more interest than I realized, among our recruiting prospects, in that game...."

Gilbert and Bradley sparked Texas to a 19-0 victory over Mississippi, igniting false hopes that 1967 would be the "Year of the 'Horns.'"

In May, the Board of Regents gave Royal a vote of confidence by extending his contract to run through Dec. 31, 1977. That made the summer a bit more pleasant for him but it didn't help anything that fall.

Texas lost its 1967 opener to USC, 17-13.

"This verifies what I've said all along, that this 'Year of the 'Horns' thing is way out of line," said Royal. "We're an average football team, at best."

When someone asked what had happened to all that vicious tackling for which Texas had been noted, Royal replied: "We graduated it."

After losing to Texas Tech and beating Oklahoma State, the Longhorns seemed destined during the first half of the Oklahoma game to lose their second straight to the Sooners. Although Oklahoma held only a 7-0 lead at halftime, the Sooners had kicked Texas all over the field.

When Bradley took a blow on the head and came out of the game during the second quarter, complaining that he was dizzy and didn't know what was going on, Royal commented: "I haven't even been hit and I don't know what's going on."

But that's when the Longhorns made that remarkable second-half recovery and salvaged a 9-7 victory.

Texas went on to defeat Arkansas, Rice, SMU and Baylor, joining Texas A&M in a tie for the conference lead. During their 24-0 conquest of Baylor, the Longhorns collected 244 yards passing—the highest total a Royal-coached team at Texas ever had gained through the air. Bradley was responsible for most of it, completing 10 passes in 21 attempts for 220 yards.

But against TCU the following week, the Longhorns tied a school record—for fewest first downs in a game, four. The Horned Frogs scored another of their famous upsets of Texas, this one by 24-17. Chris Gilbert unreeled the longest scoring run from scrimmage in Southwest Conference history, 96 yards, and then set up a second touchdown with a 61-yard romp to the TCU 1.

But except for those two long runs, Royal noted later, "we were never in the game."

The final curtain on Royal's three-year nightmare came down on Thanksgiving Day, when Texas A&M scored a 10-7 victory over the Longhorns. It was the first time the Aggies ever had beaten a Royal-coached team.

Royal was asked in the dressing room about speculation that Texas still might receive a bowl invitation.

"There'll be no bowl game for us," he declared quickly. "We're going home and go to work."

Royal savors the final moments of Texas' 21–17 victory over Notre Dame in the 1970 Cotton Bowl Classic, after his classic "4th and 2" call.

Chapter 15

RISE AND FALL

Royal's climb back to glory coincided almost exactly with the stepping down from power of his close friend, President Lyndon B. Johnson. During the early part of 1968, while Johnson was making his decision not to seek reelection, Royal was working overtime to revise and revitalize the Texas offense. He and Asst. Coach Emory Bellard, who later became head coach at Texas A&M, spent much of the 1967-68 winter developing what has since been termed the "Wondrous Wishbone" offense. Basically, it's the Split T but with the fullback a couple of steps in front of the halfbacks, producing a "Y" arrangement in the backfield.

The wonders it was to help produce were far from evident when the 1968 season opened. Texas tied the University of Houston, 20-20, and lost to Texas Tech, 22-31. But then the Longhorns started a 30-game winning streak which brought Royal two more national championships (in 1969 and 1970), another "Coach of the Year" award and the "Coach of the Decade" (1960s) honor from ABC-TV.

The phenomenal streak included that famous 15-14 "Big Shootout" victory over Arkansas in 1969, when the Longhorns captivated the entire nation—including President Richard M. Nixon. And it included the memorable 21-17 victory over Notre Dame in the 1970 Cotton Bowl Classic. In the same New Year's Day game one year later, Notre Dame ended the long winning streak by defeating Texas, 24-11.

Texas bounced right back from that to post won-lost records of 8-3 for the 1971 season and 10-1 for 1972. And Royal was most pleased that Johnson, during the four years he lived after leaving the White House, witnessed so many of those shining hours; during those four years, Royal's teams won 39 games and lost only five.

The winning streak began in 1968 with a 31-3 massacre of Oklahoma State in Austin. The next week, when Texas arrived in Dallas for the Oklahoma game, Royal crossed paths with the man who was to succeed Johnson, Richard Nixon.

"He had been campaigning up there and it turned out that I was supposed to stay in the suite where he had been staying," Royal recalled. "But they were running late and when I got there, he hadn't moved out and they said it would be a couple of hours more. The Hilton Inn people were kind of upset but I wasn't. I just told them to put my luggage somewhere and I'd move in after he left. A week or so later, I got a nice letter from Mr. Nixon apologizing."

Royal first met Nixon not long after the 1965 Orange Bowl Game, when they were both playing in a golf tournament at Marco Island, Florida.

"His locker was next to mine and I introduced myself," said Royal. "He recalled that Orange Bowl Game and I was surprised at how much he remembered about the personnel and how the game went."

But, as Royal was to learn later, Nixon was a much more ardent football fan than was Johnson.

"I don't think President Johnson really was very interested in football," said Royal. "He got interested in our team because he knew some of the players, and he knew me, and went to see our games. That will kinda make a fan out of you and make you pull for winning. But he never was interested in talking technically about the game or how it's run; he didn't care that much about it. He was interested in personalities and individuals but he wasn't interested in the game of football."

In 1968, the debut of the "Worster crowd" converted a great many ordinary citizens into football fans but Johnson, preparing to step down from the presidency, did not see the Longhorns play that year.

Steve Worster, a 204-pound tailback from Bridge City, had been one of the most highly-recruited high school stars in history. Since Royal had Gilbert and Ted Koy at halfbacks, there was a great deal of pre-season speculation on where Worster would play.

When Royal was asked about that, he replied: "He's kinda like that four hundred-pound gorilla: he'll play wherever he wants to."

Royal made sure, of course, that Worster "wanted" to play fullback. Worster won All-Conference honors at that position for three years and became All-America while setting new school records for scoring (216 points) and touchdowns (36) during his college career.

But, as it turned out, the key to that unprecedented three-year string of success was held by James Street, a junior who had played a total of only 20 minutes as a sophomore quarterback and then missed spring practice to pitch for the baseball team.

Street replaced Bradley at quarterback during the third quarter of the Texas Tech game, the second of the 1968 season. Royal moved Bradley to split end the next week and some observers became convinced he had found the combination when Bradley caught a wobbly, 4-yard touchdown pass from Street late in the fourth quarter of the Oklahoma State game. Even a 60-yard pass from Street to End Charles (Cotton) Speyrer for Texas' first touchdown somehow seemed less significant than the new alignment which the Street-to-Bradley pass indicated.

Bradley immediately went into a wild dance of ecstasy which made it clear to the 51,000 fans that he didn't mind surrendering the quarter-backing job to Street.

A week later, Street erased any doubts about his ownership of the job when he brought Texas from behind for a 26-20 victory over Oklahoma. There were only two minutes and thirty-seven seconds left to play when Street launched an 85-yard touchdown drive which overcame the Sooners' 20-19 lead.

Royal later cited that drive as a big turning point for the Longhorns that season.

"Taking a team eighty-five yards has got to do something for a boy and the team," he declared. "I *know* it does something for the coach!"

It also did something for the printers of bumper stickers, at least in the Austin area. After Street guided Texas to successive victories over Oklahoma, Arkansas and Rice, they came out with a sticker which said: "STREET FOR PRESIDENT."

The loquacious Street, when asked if he would accept the presidential nomination if it were offered, responded in atypical fashion by saying simply: "Natch."

But the shock of Street's answering such a question with only one syllable was surpassed the next week by Royal's springing a daring end-around against SMU.

On the Thursday before that game, Royal sent the squad into the dressing room—and then suddenly called back his first-string backfield and Speyrer.

"He said he had something he wanted to try," Speyrer recalled later. "We lined up and ran this end-around four or five times, just the backfield and me."

"This end-around" play was a reverse off the triple option which had been working so well. Street started around the right side, faking to the fullback and threatening to pitch to a halfback going wide. Suddenly, he did pitch—but to Speyrer, going back in the other direction, rather than to the halfback.

It almost looked as though Speyrer had "intercepted" a pitch to the halfback. Speyrer had to go deep, in order to avoid the defensive right end trying to catch the usual option play from the rear. He did, when Texas pulled the play on SMU, and Tackle Bobby Wuensch came through with a crunching blind-side block on SMU End Mike Mitchell. That was ten minutes deep in that crucial game and Speyrer went 81 yards, to the SMU 4, before he was knocked out of bounds.

The play worked better on the field, almost, than it did on the blackboard. It broke open the floodgates as Texas scored a 38-7 victory over SMU and took the inside track for the Southwest Conference championship.

While many of the fans were shocked that Royal would use such a daring play, he commented later: "I was surprised that so many people were surprised when we ran it."

That game also offered a graphic demonstration of one pet Royal theory about passing. SMU's Chuck Hixson, the nation's leading passer at that time, completed 31 of his 50 passes for 336 yards against the Longhorns. But most of them were for short yardage, and he had three intercepted. And, meanwhile, the Texas defense was holding the SMU running attack to a grand total of *minus* two yards.

Royal believes that you can give the opposition short gains on passes, it they want to rely on an aerial game, and the normal percentage of interceptions will offset many of their gains.

But he paid high tribute, the night before the SMU game, to Mustang Jerry Levias, a pass-receiving star.

"If I could have just one strep throat to hand out, I'd give it to Levias," he declared.

Texas double-teamed Levias on most plays the next day but he still caught six passes for 124 yards.

The "anti-passing" Royal used a couple of bombs to conquer Tennessee, 36-13, in the January 1, 1969, Cotton Bowl game. Street hit Speyrer with touchdown passes of 78 and 79 yards during that encounter, even while people were continuing to quote Royal's comment that "Three things can happen when you pass and two of them are bad . . . ."

While other people may have had some misconceptions about Royal's philosophy, the University of Texas Regents knew it was one they wanted to keep. Thats why they raised his salary to $35,000 at the start of the 1969 season.

Their confidence was justified by another national championship—although a series of remarkable comebacks was necessary to achieve it. Fortunately, the graduation of Gilbert was offset by the arrival on the varsity of Jim Bertelsen, the halfback whiz from Hudson, Wisconsin.

The 1969 season turned out to be one of the most eventful and dramatic not only of Royal's coaching career but in University of Texas history.

It started in controversy, when ABC-TV persuaded Texas and Arkansas—which appeared to be the class of the Southwest Conference—to switch the date of their confrontation from October 18 to December 6. Because of the money involved in a national television appearance, both schools were happy to oblige.

Texas clobbered Navy, 56-17, in the third game of the season and former President Johnson witnessed the slaughter. Most of the 65,000 other fans in the stadium did not discover his presence until halftime, when the Longhorn Band played "Ruffles and Flourishes" and "The Star-Spangled Banner" in his honor. It was the first time he had been in Memorial Stadium since November 16, 1963, his last Saturday as vice-president, when he watched Texas play TCU.

As soon as he was discovered by the multitudes, the aisle near his seat became clogged with autograph seekers. He retreated, within a few minutes, to a vacant seat among high-ranking Navy officers in an adjacent section; but the autograph seekers seemed to send in their reserves, just as the Longhorns were doing, and Johnson left during the middle of the third quarter.

He didn't miss much, because by that time the competition for his autograph had become more spirited than that on the artificial turf below.

The victory was Royal's one hundredth at Texas and his team gave him the game ball as a memento of it. Although he was most appreciative, Royal said: "I really don't find the one hundredth any more satisfying than my first one, against Georgia." He paused a moment and then added, "But I'd kinda like to win my last one."

Royal also noted again that football coaches cannot ever be completely happy.

"This is the third game in a row that we haven't been really extended," he said. "This hurts us on conditioning. And I'm worried because we haven't had one of those good ol' country gut-checks yet."

They had it the following week in Dallas, where they overcame a 14-0 Oklahoma lead to win a nationally-televised game, 27-17. Street's passing, which netted 215 yards on nine completions in eighteen attempts, failed to alter Royal's "anti-passing" image.

On Thanksgiving Day, Texas bashed A&M, 49-12, while Arkansas was running over Texas Tech, 33-0. That brought both Texas and Arkansas into their December 6 clash undefeated and untied—and, as Royal put it, made ABC-TV "look wiser than a tree full of owls."

Royal's designation of the Texas-Arkansas game as the "Big Shootout" caught on quickly. With Texas riding an 18-game winning streak and Arkansas undefeated in 15 games, football fans throughout the nation anxiously awaited the kickoff; in Austin and Fayetteville, the pressure mounted to a feverish pitch.

On the Wednesday night before the game, more than 25,000 Longhorn fans turned out for a mammoth, two-and-a-half-hour pep rally in Memorial Stadium. It featured 10 bands, a hog-calling contest, the reading of a proclamation from Governor Preston Smith urging Texas to "Hook 'em, 'Horns!" and telegrams from such celebrities as Astronaut Alan Bean, Actor Fess Parker and Dr. Denton Cooley, all Texas exes—in addition to the usual remarks from players and coaches.

Cooley produced probably the most massive groan of his heart transplant career with his telegram, which said: "Win or lose, I'm with you with all my hearts."

The gigantic, unprecedented rally heightened anticipation to the point where long distance telephone operators in Austin began answering with: "Beat Arkansas! Operator."

"One of them explained that, 'The operators in Arkansas are saying

'Beat Texas' so I guess it's all right for us to say 'Beat Arkansas!'"

The teams already were lining up for the kickoff when President Nixon's helicopter landed on the practice field just south of the stadium in Fayetteville.

"The President had better hurry," quipped a pressbox humorist, "or he won't get to see Texas' first team."

Texas had piled up so many lopsided victories that season that the starters had spent most of their time on the bench, provoking all sorts of jokes about the possibility that they would not log enough playing time to letter.

This game, however, bore little resemblance to anything that had happened before. It was one of those rare confrontations which received a tremendous buildup—and then made the advance billing seem insufficient.

During the first three quarters, Texas was frustrated completely. The Longhorns lost the ball on four fumbles and two pass interceptions while Arkansas was fashioning a 14-0 lead.

Suddenly, on the first play of the fourth quarter, Street dropped back to pass but was flushed out of the pocket by the fire-breathing Razorbacks. He tucked the ball under his arm and started running. One defender bounced off him at the thirty, and another at the twenty. And then he was all alone in the end zone, and Texas fans all across the nation were going wild.

Street kept the ball and dived inside tackle for a 2-point conversion that cut the Arkansas lead to 14-8 and put the Longhorns back in the ball game. It was an uphill climb all the way, and when they reached the Arkansas 43 with only four minutes and forty-seven seconds left to play, facing fourth down and three, the odds against them seemed all but impossible to overcome.

Street went over to the bench to confer with Royal, while fans from coast to coast gnawed fingernails.

The play called by "Daring Darrell" sent shock waves throughout the football world. His decision, he recalled later, was based partly on what turned out to be false information but resulted primarily from a hunch.

"I never considered punting," he said, looking back. "I knew we didn't have time to do that and then move the ball back down there. I just thought it was time to swing from the floor. Every now and then, you have to just play a hunch without using logic or reason."

Some logic was involved, of course. At halftime, Royal had asked End Randy Peschel if the halfback was coming up too fast for him to block when Texas ran the triple option to his side.

"He said yes," Royal recalled. "That meant that, if he was coming up that fast, Peschel could get behind him for a pass."

Partly as a result of that, Royal instructed Street to call "53 Veer Pass."

Street started back but, about the time he took his first step, the full impact hit him; he did a double take, turning back to Royal.

"Are you sure?" he asked.

Royal assured him, most emphatically, that he was sure.

Peschel was just as surprised as Street to hear they would try a long pass on fourth down.

"If you can't get open, cut back or do something to get us enough for a first down," Street told Peschel. "But if you *can* get behind 'em, run like hell!"

Defensive Backs Jerry Moore and Dennis Berner both dropped back to cover Peschel.

"I got a good step on 'em when I first came out," Peschel reported later, "but they both caught me while the ball was in the air."

Street threw it perfectly. The ball barely escaped Moore's hands as Peschel caught it, just as Berner reached him. Peschel came down on the Arkansas 13, clutching the ball to his chest for a 44-yard gain.

The Longhorns on the bench were still wild with joy when Street sent Koy slashing 11 yards through tackle on the next play. Then Bertelsen crashed his way through the same spot for the last two yards and the touchdown. Happy Feller kicked the game-winning extra point to make it 15-14, with three minutes and fifty-eight seconds left on the clock.

In storybook fashion, Arkansas came slashing back. Bill Montgomery drove the Razorbacks back upfield to the Texas 39, with 1:22 left to play. From there, he tried a deep pass to John Rees and Texas' Tom Campbell (son of Coach Mike) intercepted it at the Longhorn 21.

Back in the locker room, the Longhorns calmed down long enough for Koy to lead them in "The Lord's Prayer." Then President Nixon came in to present a presidential plaque recognizing them as the nation's Number One football team—a move which drew howls of protest from Penn State. The protests prompted President Nixon later to send a similar plaque to Penn State Coach Joe Paterno, citing his team for having the nation's longest winning streak.

The television cameras came into the Texas locker room for the plaque presentation.

This was one of the greatest games of all time," Nixon declared. "The wire services will name Texas the Number One team and this is a great honor in the one hundredth year of college football. The fact that you won a tough game and the fact that you didn't lose your cool and didn't quit makes you deserving of Number One."

Royal thanked the President and said, "I know I speak for all our squad and coaches when I say that when the President of the United States takes time to come to our dressing room, it is a great honor."

Despite the fantastic finish, Royal felt the Longhorns had played poorly and that he personally had failed to prepare them properly.

"In fact, I think we did a sorrier job in that victory—which probably is the biggest we've ever had since I've been at Texas, based on what was at stake—than we did in that 1958 Sugar Bowl loss to Ole Miss.

"I just don't think we did a good job, at all. I didn't think so coming back on the plane, I didn't think so when I saw the films and I don't think so yet," he declared more than three years later.

"We had one great play, and we had a gutty call, but the rest of it stunk. And that was a *lucky* call, I guess. I felt like we had to do something. If we made four yards and a routine first down, I felt like we'd still lose because the clock was working against us. And I didn't feel like we were going to take it down there at a snail's pace and score. It was obvious we were off-key that day. It was now or never. You just kinda go by hunches, and sometimes they pay off.

"But that call was also based on some bad information. When I saw the film, I found that the reason Peschel couldn't get out to block that halfback was that they were holding him up on the line of scrimmage and he was 'way late getting off the line; it was not because the halfback was coming up fast. The halfback actually covered him on that pass and was in pretty darned good position. And their safety came over so there were three of them right there in a wad, going up for that pass.

"I thought it was a highly unlikely call, and sometimes you've got to break your pattern. People have the conception of us that we won't ever do anything like that. They're right when they say we won't do anything like that *most* of the time.

"In the 1972 A&M game, on fourth and one, we threw a pass—in the rain—and we got a touchdown out of it. If we'd made a yard and a first down, I don't think we'd have scored. It makes you feel good when you hit one right, but you're equally dejected when you call one wrong, when you miss one of those two-foot putts. You feel like a dog, then.

"You don't work any harder for one game than you do for others but sometimes you just happen to hit right. You have your ups and downs. Some days you can answer mail better than on others; some days you can make better talks to booster clubs than you can on others; some days you can communicate with your squad better than on others, and some days you can communicate with your wife better than on others.

"We've had some sorry games and if I'm going to take all those pats on the back and feel like we were right on target on the good ones, I've got to feel like there are times when we're 'way off target and I deserve the blame. Sometimes you get to feeling too chesty and there's nothing like a good thrashing to get your feet back on the ground.

"Lucky—man, we were lucky in that 15-14 game! James goes back to throw a pass and can't find a receiver open, and he's rushed, so he puts the ball down and runs. One or two guys fall down and he scores standing up. It's supposed to be a loss—and it's a touchdown.

"And then we throw that pass through a keyhole on fourth and three. We couldn't go back and duplicate that play one time out of twenty even you; it was almost like it was predestined, like it was already set and this is the way it was going to be.

"We just didn't play well. Arkansas outplayed us in that football game. I thought they were better-prepared emotionally and better-prepared from a technical standpoint," Royal declared.

But Arkansas did not have James Street. And Street pulled a couple of other outstanding plays that night, when the Longhorns flew home to a jubilant welcome which got slightly out of hand.

Just as the plane landed in Austin, a voice came over its public address system: "This is the captain speaking. Congratulations to you boys. You all did well. Especially the offense. However, the defense was a little shaky at times—so you'd better straighten up before you play Notre Dame in the Cotton Bowl!"

By the time he finished that speech, most of the players realized that Street had commandeered the stewardesses' microphone; his remarks provoked a huge gale of laughter.

After they landed, the Longhorns found themselves stymied by a throng of about 15,000 celebrants. Before the pilot could taxi the plane to the terminal, the crowd surged onto the field and surrounded it, forcing him to stop the engines. The buses which were there to pick up the players finally went to meet the plane, still about 100 yards from the nearest gate; still, the wild crowd kept the team from getting off the plane for more than thirty minutes.

The first few players who tried to leave were jostled so much that they retreated and hurried back into the plane, lest they be killed with kindness.

But, once again, Street came to the rescue. He and Wuensch went to the plane's front door and stood there waving the "Hook 'em, 'Horns" sign to the overly-enthusiastic mob. While the fans yelled themselves hoarse, most of the other players outflanked them and escaped through the plane's rear door.

After the crowd failed to heed their pleas to clear a path, Street and Wuensch finally decided to make a run for it. One of the fans, apparently well-oiled, actually tried to tackle Street but Wuensch then came to the quarterback's rescue, as he had a number of times in Fayetteville, and knocked the guy loose.

The celebrations in Austin went on and on, with a jubilant atmosphere lingering throughout the entire city for days. But the next Wednesday, while he was in New York, Royal received a shocking telephone call which suddenly turned the roses into ashes.

(Photo by James Laughead)

Royal's joy knew no bounds as his players carried him off the field after their 12–7 victory over Mississippi in the 1962 Cotton Bowl Classic. Royal was named "Coach of the Year" for 1961.

Chapter 16

CHAMP OF CHAMPS

On Tuesday night, December 9, 1969, Royal and his tricaptains—
Street, Koy and Linebacker Glen Halsell—appeared at the National
Football Foundation and Hall of Fame's annual banquet in New York's
Waldorf-Astoria to receive the MacArthur Bowl trophy, symbolic of
another national championship.

It was a gala evening. It began with the Texans chatting informally
with President Nixon, who also was being honored at the banquet. It
ended at the famed Bachelors III night club, where Koy, Street and
Halsell visited with Joe Namath and the ex-Longhorns on the New York
Jets—Pete Lammons, George Sauer, John Elliott and Jim Hudson. Bill
Bradley, who had become the Philadelphia Eagles' safety man, also was
on hand for the reunion.

Wednesday, the tricaptains went to Washington as honor guests at the
weekly luncheon of the Texas congressional delegation. House Speaker
John McCormack, Majority Leader Carl Albert and Minority Leader
Gerald Ford all came by to pay their respects to the nation's Number One
football team.

Royal had planned on going to Washington, too, but that morning he
received a telephone call from Dr. Charles A. LeMaistre, chancellor of the
University of Texas and a medical doctor. Dr. LeMaistre said that
Steinmark was being taken to the M.D. Anderson Hospital and Tumor
Institute in Houston. X-rays, he explained, indicated that what Steinmark
had thought was a deep bruise in his thigh apparently was a tumor.

"Suddenly," said Royal, "that trophy didn't seem nearly as important
as it had just before that phone call . . . ."

Royal flew to Houston. He was with Steinmark when the doctors told
him they would have to operate and, if a biopsy showed a malignant
tumor, immediate amputation of his left leg would be necessary. There
was a possibility, they explained, that it might not be a tumor—or that it
might be benign.

Six days after he had played against Arkansas, Steinmark's left leg
was amputated at the hip. Expressions of sympathy, and of admiration
for his courage, poured in from people throughout the nation, including
President Nixon.

Steinmark announced that he had three immediate goals: to attend the Cotton Bowl Game, to be walking on an artificial leg when he received his football award at the team banquet on January 12, and to enroll in school again in February. The courage and the determination he demonstrated in achieving all three goals earned him tons of admiration and respect.

While Steinmark was learning to walk again, his teammates began getting ready to play Notre Dame—which had accepted a bowl invitation for the first time since 1925, when the Four Horsemen rode roughshod over Stanford in the Rose Bowl, 27-10.

And Royal, during one of those practice sessions a few days before Christmas, spiked recurring rumors that his second national championship might prompt him to retire from coaching.

He was interviewed by a *Dallas Morning News* writer as the two sat on top of Royal's 30-foot high, portable observation tower astride the 50-yard line in Memorial Stadium. Sunlight bathed the artificial turf and, in the background, jackhammers ripped relentlessly into the historic pressbox. The pressbox was being demolished as the first step in the construction of the upper deck and the classroom-office building which would support it. Even before that project was completed, the athletic facilities at the University of Texas had advanced remarkably from the goatheads and cubbyholes Royal found there at first.

He kept his eyes glued constantly on a passing drill that was in progress while he was being interviewed. Occasionally, he would shout at one of the passers, "Under-thrown!" or "That's an interception—lead him more!" or "That's it, that's the way to throw it!"

He seemed to be enjoying himself immensely, and he was. At long last, he had taken a close look at himself, at his work and his ambitions; and he had decided that this, coaching football, was what he really wanted to do.

"I intend to keep on doing it as long as I enjoy it," he said.

He added that his second national championship in six years had helped him to realize that he also had enjoyed the years in between, despite those 6-4 records during three of them.

Retirement rumors had cropped up after that 1963 championship season, based on the idea that he might want to step out of active coaching while he was on top and continue merely as director of athletics. There were suspicions, both in 1963 and 1969, that some of the rumors might have been originated by rival coaches, either as wishful thinking or perhaps in an effort to hamper his recruiting.

"I was just forty years old after that '63 season and felt I was too young to retire," said Royal. "But I thought that when I did retire, it would be great to go out after winning a national championship. So I did sorta have the idea in the back of my mind that if I ever won another, I'd probably get out of coaching.

"But now, after this season, I've had to take a close look at the situation—and I'm more settled now on staying in coaching than I have been at any time since 1963. I've decided that what happens during the last three months of my coaching career really is not all that important. After all, I'm going to be judged on my entire career, and not just on my last season—so it doesn't matter so much whether I go out after a big winning season.

"If the last three months is that important," he added, "what I've been doing here for thirteen years is pretty flimsy."

Royal also declared firmly that he had no intention of ever entering politics, despite such suggestions from a few of his friends. He contended that his knowledge was limited almost entirely to football and that circumstances, ironically, tended to reinforce that situation every year despite his great curiousity about many things.

He noted that football had given him opportunities to meet many interesting, well-informed people, from presidents of the United States on down—but almost invariably, they wanted to talk with him about nothing but football, giving him little or no chance to learn about them and their activities.

"I certainly don't resent this at all, and I appreciate their interest," he said. "But at parties, for instance, if I walk up to a group of people, no matter what they're talking about, they'll switch the conversation quickly to football. I enjoy it but it does restrict the flow of information, so that you reach the age of forty-five and football is all you know anything about. You can't 'pick' other people to find out about their activities, and finally you forget how to."

Royal admitted that he had been able to learn a little about the problems of the presidency during his visits with President Johnson, which then were beginning to grow more frequent. He also had managed to get an insight into the motion picture business when he and Edith were entertained by Mr. and Mrs. Gregory Peck in Hollywood. They had met a few weeks earlier at a Headliners Club Awards Party in Austin. When Edith mentioned then that they were going to California for a "Coach of the Year" clinic, the Pecks insisted that they call them while they were in Los Angeles.

They did—and the visit produced one of Royal's most interesting experiences.

"They spent the entire day with us and took us to a lot of fun places," Royal recalled. "But what I enjoyed most was going out to the set of the movie, *To Kill a Mockingbird*, and having Gregory Peck explain everything to us. He went into great detail on the filming process. And it was especially interesting since we'd lived in Mississippi and that movie captured many aspects of life in the Deep South."

Such incidents, Royal noted, help compensate for his usual steady diet of football, golf, football, country-western music and football.

When January 1, 1970, rolled around, football appeared to be uppermost in the minds of people all over the country, and in all walks of life—including President Nixon and former President Johnson. But perhaps no one was looking forward more eagerly to Texas' Cotton Bowl clash with Notre Dame than was Steinmark.

"I felt that Freddie's coming to the Cotton Bowl Game was his and his doctors' decision," said Royal. "If he wanted to come, there was no question but what he was in the family. Yet, all of us would have understood if he hadn't wanted to come. My only concern was for Freddie. I was delighted that he wanted to come and I think all of us got a lift from his wanting to be there."

Ted Koy agreed, commenting later: "When Freddie came into the dressing room before the game, it picked us all up. He didn't have to say anything. Just being there was communicating enough."

Although it was the first time most of the players had seen Steinmark since his operation, they purposely did not make a big deal of it, Royal noted.

"They just came by, one by one, and said 'hello' to him," said Royal.

And they also dedicated the game to him.

Steinmark, accompanied by the Rev. Fred Bomar of Austin, a Catholic priest who spent an enormous amount of time with him throughout his ordeal, stood on the sidelines during the game—preferring his crutches to a chair.

The game turned out to be an incredible reproduction of the Arkansas cliff-hanger, even to the final interception.

Texas spotted the Fighting Irish a 10-0 lead before launching the first of three long touchdown drives and was trailing, 10-7, at the half. The fourth quarter was five minutes old before the Longhorns gained a 14-10 lead, and that was short-lived. It lasted only three minutes, in fact, before Notre Dame went ahead again, 17-14, with six minutes and fifty-two seconds left to play.

That's when the indomitable Street cranked up the Longhorns for what turned out to be a 76-yard, 17-play drive which had to survive two fourth down situations. The first of those came at the Irish 20, with 4:26 left on the clock; on fourth and two, Koy took a pitch around left end for two yards, almost exactly. They had to measure it before awarding Texas the first down.

Koy tried the same play again and lost a yard. Bertelsen hit the middle of the line for four, then went around right end for five more.

Fourth down and two, once more. Two minutes and twenty-six seconds left to play. A capacity crowd of 73,000 in the Cotton Bowl and a nationwide television audience all on the brink of a mass coronary attack. Street went over to the bench to get Royal's decision.

"Left Eighty-nine Out," said Royal, "and force the corner."

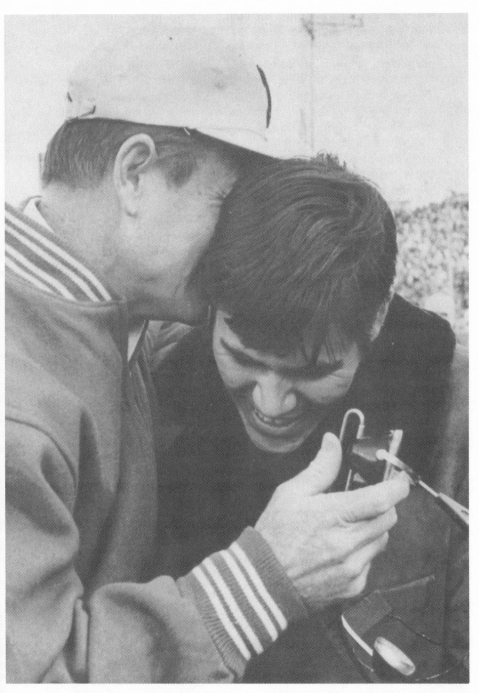

Royal gives the good word to Freddie Steinmark on the sideline at the 1970 Cotton Bowl Classic, where Texas came from behind for a 21-17 victory.

That meant to look first for an opportunity to keep the ball and run but, if the run wasn't open, to throw a short pass to Speyrer.

In the huddle, Street told his team: "This might be our last play of the season, so let's make it a good one."

Street took the snap and began running to the left. When the outside linebacker crashed through, he put on the brakes and threw the ball.

An Irish defender was sticking to Speyrer like a shadow but the pass came in low. Speyrer dived and scooped it to his chest just before he hit the ground on the two-yard line.

Three plays later, from the one, Worster made a great fake, Peschel got a tremendous block and Billy Dale rammed his way over for the winning touchdown, with one minute and eight seconds left to play.

But the 21-17 victory still wasn't safe. Notre Dame Quarterback Joe Theismann threw a couple of passes that put the Irish on the Texas 39-yard line with thirty-eight seconds left to play. Then he tried another—and the same Tom Campbell, of Arkansas interception fame, was there to pick it off. Campbell returned it to the 23.

As he was knocked out of bounds, fists started flying and some of those on the sidelines—including photographers and sportswriters—were caught in the middle of the action. When one of them broke away and ran over to a policeman, asking him to break it up, the officer reportedly replied: "Are you crazy? There's no way I'm jumping in there!"

In the emotion-charged dressing room, Royal gasped for breath as he held the game ball and told his squad: "It would be an understatement to try to tell you how proud I am of you. If I try to talk too long, I'm going to choke up. But we've got a guy we love a lot—and Freddie, here it is for you!"

With that, he gave the game ball to Steinmark and the celebration got into full swing.

Former President Johnson was among the first fans to reach the dressing room. In a brief speech, he told the Longhorns: "It was a great privilege for everyone to see these two great football teams today. It was inspiring to see young men fighting for every inch of ground. I was proud of both teams but I was especially proud of Darrell Royal and every man on his team. Notre Dame fought to the last play and we just had a little luck. God bless you all."

About that time, President Nixon telephoned Royal to congratulate him.

"I'm glad we didn't cause you to be embarrassed by your selection of us as Number One," Royal told him.

"I wouldn't have been embarrassed even had you lost," the President replied, "because it was a great, hard-fought game by both teams and you played like champions."

When someone asked Royal if President Nixon called from

In a call that shocked sports fans over the nation, with his team facing fourth down and two and only 2:26 left on the clock, Royal told James Street to throw a pass. Texas was trailing Notre Dame, 14–17, but Street's pass to Cotton Speyrer took the Longhorns to the two-yard line and set up the winning touchdown.

Former President Johnson visited the Longhorn locker room to congratulate Quarterback James Street and Royal after Texas defeated Notre Dame, 21–17, in the 1970 New Year's Day Classic at Dallas.

Washington or from San Clemente, he laughed and said, "I don't know—I didn't ask him a hell of a lot of questions!"

And when a sportswriter asked, "What led to that fourth and two call just before your last touchdown?", Royal quipped, "About a sixty-yard drive!"

After the laughter subsided, Royal went on to explain that the play was a run-or-pass option and he had hoped the Notre Dame defense would drop back enough to let Street run instead of throw.

But Royal certainly had no complaints. As a matter of fact, he concluded the dressing room interviews by declaring,"If anybody wants anything from me, this would be a great time to ask me for it. I think I'd have trouble saying 'no' to anyone right now!"

Before Steinmark left the dressing room, he was asked if he had grown tired during the game.

"No," he replied, "things were so exciting that I really didn't have a chance to get tired. That was some game! It was great. But I never lost faith in these guys. Win, lose or draw, this team is always in there. That's the kind of guys we have."

Steinmark later received the Philadelphia Sports Writers Association's "Most Courageous Athlete of the Year" award. When he accepted it, he declared, "You just have to be realistic and take what comes along in life."

What came along in his life surely must have been a little easier to take as a result of the tremendous, standing ovation he received at the Longhorns' football banquet almost two weeks after the Cotton Bowl Game.

Although the 1970 Hula Bowl Game was dedicated to Steinmark, he passed up an opportunity to visit Honolulu for it; he wanted, instead, to stay home and practice walking on his artificial leg. He must have broken all existing records for learning to use an artificial limb but he wanted desperately to walk across that stage on January 12th.

An overflow crowd of more than 4,500 people attended that unforgettable banquet in Austin's Municipal Auditorium. Instead of the usual stuffy banquet atmosphere, it was a happy, informal western barbecue. About 3,000 persons paid $3.50 each to serve themselves, with paper plates, to barbecue, beans and potato salad, while another 1,500 crowded the balcony at $1.50 each just to watch.

Peschel gave the invocation, which included these words: "Lord, help us all to be as brave as Freddie Steinmark."

Cactus Pryor, Austin humorist who appears as the co-host on Royal's weekly television program during the football season, served as master of ceremonies.

"This is a 'fourth and two' barbecue," he declared. "It all started on a cold, rainy day in Fayetteville, Arkansas, when Texas faced a crucial fourth-down-and-two situation with just a few minutes left while trailing

Arkansas, 14-8. Coach Darrell Royal called Quarterback James Street over to the sideline and said, 'James, this year I think we ought to have a barbecue.' And James replied, 'Coach, are you sure?'"

Pryor said the long pass Royal ordered in that situation was "the wildest call since Billy Graham telephoned Zsa Zsa Gabor." And he added that one of the Longhorns' greatest thrills came when President Nixon showed up in their dressing room after that game to present a plaque "making Texas Number One and Pennsylvania Democratic."

All the drama and excitement and pathos of that memorable season came to a climax when Steinmark received his letter award. Introducing the players in alphabetical order, Royal passed over Linebacker Scott Henderson's name when he first came to it. When he got to Steinmark, he explained that the two were such close friends that they wanted to appear together.

Then Steinmark began walking across the stage, slowly but surely, on his artificial leg and with the aid of a cane. Henderson walked at the same pace, a few steps behind him, just in case he started to fall or needed help.

Steinmark didn't need any help. The people who needed help were the 4,500 who watched. They—including big, rugged football players and cynical, hardened newsmen—stood and applauded for several minutes, crying unashamedly and all but taking the roof off that big auditorium.

There wasn't much left to say after that. Mrs. Lyndon B. Johnson presented the *Associated Press* national championship trophy to the team, without a word. Her husband, described by Pryor as "a prominent rancher," was introduced but also declined an opportunity to speak.

That, of course, came after Steinmark accepted his letter. And his dramatic performance apparently left even the former President speechless—perhaps for the first time in his career.

Chapter 17

RUFFLES, FLOURISHES
AND FLOWERS

Although President Johnson never shared Royal's enthusiasm for golf, the two did play together a number of times—especially while they were taking February vacations in Acapulco during 1971 and 1972.

During one of their games, Johnson putted to within about two feet of the cup and the other two members of their foursome immediately tagged it a "gimme," urging the former president to pick up his ball.

"Let him putt it out," said Royal, laconically. "That helps build character."

A faint grin crossed Johnson's face as he got over the ball and muttered, "That's probably why Royal wins so many football games—he won't give anybody anything!"

Whatever the reason, Royal was rapidly becoming one of the winningest coaches in college football history. In 1973, the National Collegiate Sports Services announced that Texas had been the most successful college team in the land during the previous five years, winning 45 games while losing four and tying one for a .910 percentage. Penn State was a close second, winning 47 and losing five for a .904 batting average.

Royal's Longhorns won all 10 of their regular season games in 1970. Included was a devastating 42-7 romp over Arkansas in "Big Shootout II" at Austin.

"Although we'd played such a sorry game in beating Arkansas the year before," said Royal, "I thought we had 'em zeroed in and were right on the bull's-eye in 1970. We probably had as little confusion as we've ever had, during that game."

That one also had been moved to the end of the season for national television purposes. And a great season it was, for the Longhorns. In addition to the new records established by Worster, Happy Feller posted new NCAA marks of 128 extra points for his career and 185 points by place-kicking during three years. Texas led the nation in scoring, with an average of 41.2 points per game, and in rushing, with an average of 374.5 yards per game.

But then Notre Dame came back to the Cotton Bowl to score that 24-11 victory which clipped Texas' consecutive victory string at 30 games.

In 1971, Texas lost to Oklahoma and Arkansas but bounced back to score five straight victories and became the first school ever to win four Southwest Conference championships in a row. Quarterback Donnie Wigginton tied a school record by scoring 14 touchdowns—thanks in large part to Tackle Jerry Sisemore, a consensus All-America selection both that year and again in 1972. And Bertelsen wound up his brilliant career as Texas' second greatest rusher of all time, with a career total of 2,510 yards to Gilbert's 3,231.

The Longhorns also became the first school ever to play in four consecutive Cotton Bowl Classics—but that proved to be a most unpleasant experience. Penn State finally got its revenge for that 1969 plaque by whipping Texas, 30-6, in what Royal feels was one of his most "inadequate" coaching jobs.

"We were not prepared for the type of defense they played," he declared. "We were confused. We had players with good ability who didn't know where to go—and that was my fault. Penn State changed its pattern to a defense we hadn't anticipated and hadn't worked on; when you're going into a bowl game, you ought to anticipate better what the other team is going to do. And we should have had a better offensive plan for that game; we just didn't hit it right."

Nevertheless, these were mostly days of great glory for Royal—and no one seemed to enjoy them more than LBJ.

The first time Royal was interviewed for this book, in December of 1972, he said he did not want to talk about his friendship with President Johnson. One of the main reasons for that friendship, he felt, was the fact that he always had respected the former president's desire for privacy. But after LBJ's death the next month, Royal felt free to discuss their relationship.

"This would have been the third year for us to go to Acapulco with President and Mrs. Johnson," Royal said, shortly after Johnson's death.

"We always stayed down there at a place that belonged to a former president of Mexico, Miguel Aleman. It was built on a hillside, sort of like a motel, with the bedrooms spread out—but it definitely wasn't a motel. It houses about eight couples. We played golf down there, and went swimming, and loafed on the beach; everybody just did whatever they wanted to do, and it was great.

"The first time we went down there, Mollie Parnis, the dress designer, was there, and Mr. and Mrs. George Brown, and Mr. and Mrs. Roy Butler, and Frank Erwin, and Jean Vanderbilt, and Mr. and Mrs. Tom Frost.

"President Johnson had some paper swim suits there for people who had forgotten to bring their own swim suits; they were really unusual, and a lot stronger than you'd think, for paper. He loved to get out in the water and wade around. Some of the people, including Mrs. Johnson, would water ski. It was real vacationing. If you wanted to go take a nap, you'd go take a nap. Everybody did whatever they wanted to do.

"But I always wanted to be downstairs when anything was going on; there was no way I could go up there and take a nap when something was happening. Now, if everybody takes off and goes to their rooms, I can go up and go to sleep. But I was always hanging around . . . .

"President Johnson didn't talk to me a lot about politics but I heard a lot of politics talked because I was around people, with him, who were highly knowledgeable politically—people like Tommy Corcoran, Speaker McCormack, Frank Erwin, George Brown, Mollie Parnis . . . .

"Invariably, there was a lot of political talk if you were around him for any extended period of time. But when those conversations took place, I was just like a piece of furniture, so far as participating in them is concerned. I was 'way out of my league, and I knew it. I just didn't participate because I knew I wasn't qualified to. I was like a lost ball in tall weeds. And I'm sure they must have realized it.

"Oh, I was included, and I was allowed to listen, and I never did feel uncomfortable. But there were a lot of times they were talking about things I really didn't understand; I didn't know the background, and they'd leave out a lot of the background because they all knew it so well. I'd get lost. But some of the things they said were really interesting—just unbelievably intriguing—to sit there and hear.

"Usually, when I talked with President Johnson, it was about such things as Mrs. Johnson's flowers, or maybe a golf game. He'd really kid me about golf. He was a great kidder, and he kidded me all the time.

"But he had a great influence on my life, really.

"He always impressed me as a guy with excellent judgment—good horse sense. He was always talking about 'Mister Sam.' And he said once that one of the things he always remembered most about Speaker Sam Rayburn was that when someone recommended someone to Mister Rayburn, and told him about all the degrees and everything the guy had, he'd always come back and ask, 'But what kind of judgment does he have?'

"President Johnson told me," said Royal, "that Mister Sam said he wouldn't give a damn for any man who didn't have good judgment. He didn't care how many degrees he had, or how many academic honor societies he belonged to, he'd just say he wanted to know about his judgment. And that's the way President Johnson felt.

"If a man had good judgment, he didn't have to have a lot of rank and smell, so far as President Johnson was concerned. He didn't have to have any degrees or belong to any societies. But he felt that if a man didn't have good judgment, he wasn't worth a damn.

"Judgment was always a big thing with President Johnson, and I think he always tried to surround himself with people who had good judgment," said Royal. "He had a very delicate feel for judgment, himself—as to how strong he should word something, or when he should pull up. He had a good feel for how to manipulate and how to deal with people. He was a master of 'one-on-one'—you get him with one other person, or a small group, and he could sell almost anything."

Perhaps one reason President Johnson and Royal became so close was that neither had anything to sell the other.

"He sure loved to ride around that ranch and look at those animals and those trees, and the wildlife and the flowers," said Royal. "He'd kinda make a joke about the flowers. He'd say, 'Well, we gotta have these for Bird; can't put any cattle out there 'cause we gotta save those flowers for Bird.'

"He always sounded kinda sarcastic when he talked about 'these are Bird's flowers,' but you could tell that he loved 'em. He'd tell you that 'Bird' wouldn't let 'em put any sheep in there, or let 'em mow it—but he'd always take you to see those pastures, and he loved 'em.

"I've always had a little bit of a complex over my ability to read, and to comprehend reading, and I know my grammar is not exactly right all the time," said Royal. "I've never been a guy who could sit down and take an aptitude test and do well on it. I've always felt I was a little bit shy in the intellectual field. I had known I was incompetent in some of these areas, but being around President Johnson and hearing the things he said, especially about this business of judgment, gave me a little more confidence in my position.

"I felt incompetent in some areas—not in the football area, or in dealing with boosters, or the administration, or the Longhorn Club, or alumni, or in dealing with the coaching staff or the football team. I never have had any moist palms over doing that type of thing. But I just look around me, right and left, and see people that I consider to be smarter than I am—so far as formal education is concerned, *much* smarter. As a matter of fact, so far as college graduates are concerned, I'm probably below average.

"But I do feel I have a little judgment and I can deal with people and communicate with them," said Royal. "As President Johnson said, 'Come, let us reason together.' I put a lot of stock in that. Let us reason together. If you've got a difference, if you'll sit down with a fair-minded and open-minded person, if you'll spend just a little time talking about it, one on one, I think you can come out good friends working together, arm in arm, and go get a job done—even though you went in with a disagreement.

"That has really influenced me—President Johnson's thinking along that line. And the idea of not being so proud, and so full of ego that you wouldn't approach a guy and say, 'Come visit me and let's talk about it.' That's no sign of weakness—to sit down and reason together. It's a sign of stupidity to be so stubborn that you don't even want to sit down and talk with a guy because he disagrees with you."

Royal remembers that President Johnson had a "pleasing type of humor."

"The person he was kidding and razzing liked it," said Royal. "You felt privileged when he did it. He did it in such a way that you could tell he really liked you . . . .

"He was a warm, wonderful person and I was fortunate enough to see a side of him that few people got to see. I learned from him that you can be a common man—and, at the same time, be a great man. I was relaxed when I was with him, but I was also awed by him. Our relationship was really just a 'spit and whittle' sort of thing. Actually, our friendship was kinda surprising. All I ever did was vote for him and like him.

"But, Lord, I enjoyed riding with him over that ranch. I think each tree had a special meaning for him.

"He was a big Bertelsen fan and we flew up to Hudson, Wisconsin, one time for 'Jim Bertelsen Day.' President Johnson slept most of the way up there, but then his adrenalin got to flowing and he talked all the way back. We didn't get back to Austin until about three a.m., and he had to leave about six o'clock that morning, but it didn't seem to bother him."

Early during the 1972 season, LBJ asked Royal to bring his tricaptains—Sisemore, Lowry and Randy Braband—to the LBJ Ranch for lunch, and also invited Julius Whittier and Leaks.

"We drove all around the ranch, of course, and you didn't have to waste any time wondering where to sit when you were with President Johnson," said Royal. "He'd say, 'Now, you sit over there close to the food and, Roosevelt, you come sit here by me because I've got some questions to ask you.'"

Johnson encouraged Leaks and Whittier, both blacks, to follow the example of U.S. Rep. Barbara Jordan of Houston, who had earned great respect as a state senator before being elected to Congress. And he said they should encourage other young blacks to follow in her footsteps.

According to Royal, LBJ felt that Barbara Jordan had "hung the moon."

"He thought her thinking was right and that she was highly capable," Royal recalled. "He used her as an example when he talked to young blacks, and told them they ought to be striving to be like her."

Royal feels that Johnson had quite an impact on his life, especially in regard to his own feelings about blacks.

"I think I've always had, basically, a lot of compassion and feeling for the blacks," said Royal. "But it's like President Johnson told me: he said, 'You know, I never had thought I was prejudiced, and I still don't believe I was, but I just wasn't as concerned about their problems as I should have been.'

"That's what got me to thinking. I hadn't done anything to hurt 'em—but neither had I done anything to help 'em. Any fair-minded person would say that things had not been fair, and I knew they hadn't been fair. I knew blacks weren't being treated equally and I knew they weren't being given an equal chance. But I really hadn't worried about it, 'til then.

"I wasn't doing anything to *keep* them from having an equal chance—but I wasn't doing anything to help 'em *get* an equal chance," said Royal. "And if I had anything to be regretful about so far as the blacks were concerned, that was it—I just wasn't concerned soon enough about trying to help them. But I don't have any guilt, because I certainly did not do anything to hurt them.

"I have tried to help them, since then—partly just by talking to people, and trying to convince them that the blacks haven't had an equal chance. I feel like they need more equality; I don't think we're there yet. I don't feel they have the same opportunity that a white has, even when they're just as capable.

"That feeling came partly from spending a lot of time with President Johnson," said Royal. "If there's one thing he talked on, during the time I was with him, more than anything else, it was the race situation. Equal opportunity. The deprived. For many years, the deprived. Far too long, the deprived. This entered into our conversation a lot of the time when we were together."

Once, at the LBJ Ranch, Johnson introduced Royal to Mack Hannah, a Houston businessman and a black who had been his close personal friend for many years. And Royal cringed as they laughed about meeting secretly in earlier years, when it was not fashionable for a white and a black to be seen together in public.

The last time Royal saw Johnson was at a civil rights seminar on the University of Texas campus, in December of 1972. But his last conversation with the former president took place on the telephone not long after that 1973 Cotton Bowl victory over Alabama.

"I get the feeling," Johnson told Royal, "that you and Edith are waiting for an invitation before you'll come out here to see me. But I want you to call me just like you'd call your momma, and say, 'We're coming out to see you.' If I'm busy, or have to be somewhere else, I'll just say so and we can make it another time. But I don't want you waiting for an invitation. I really think we ought to get together more often."

Royal was driving between Conroe and Houston on Jan. 22, 1973, when he heard a news bulletin on his car radio that Johnson had died of a heart attack. The highly successful football coach, who once had hitch-hiked from Hollis, Oklahoma, to Childress, Texas, just to catch a glimpse of a President of the United States, immediately drove back to Austin.

That night, he was among other close friends of Lyndon Baines Johnson who spent two-hour shifts standing near the casket of the former president, lying in state at the LBJ Library. And he had a little trouble keeping his eyes dry as he stood there, thanking those who came to pay their last respects to a great champion of civil rights.

Freddie Steinmark and Royal presented an autographed football to President Nixon at the White House in 1970, shortly after Defensive Back Steinmark had part of his leg removed due to cancer.

(Photo by Bob Jackson)

Playing in the Pro-Am at the 1970 Byron Nelson Classic, Royal hit such a great golf shot, it almost put him into orbit.

Chapter 18

STRANGE IMAGE

One of the great foibles of modern communications is illustrated dramatically by the false image many people seem to have of Darrell Royal, on two counts. They think he hates (1) passing, and (2) blacks—not necessarily in that order.

The facts prove them wrong on both counts. But the myths persist, despite the fact that he has become one of the most publicized men in America.

When he throws a fourth down pass to beat Arkansas, or Notre Dame, or some other team—even before a nationwide television audience—the idea that he is "ground-bound" refuses to fade. Its failure to do so remains a great mystery—but it is one which Royal is happy to exploit. He knows better than anyone else that when you pass, three things can happen—and *one* of them is *good*. He merely takes a different approach in advertising, encouraging many of his opponents to get lulled into complacency which frequently contributes to their defeat.

"You play percentages, but you can't get to the point where you absolutely play percentages," said Royal. "If you do that, the other side knows what you're going to do—because they also know the percentages. We've thrown from our own end zone and we've thrown on fourth down. Sometimes, you just have to break the pattern so the other side won't know what you're going to do. But there have been many times when we have played the percentages, even knowing that the other side *knew* that's what we were doing."

Royal understands football percentages. What he does not understand are the percentages which cause him to be pictured as a "racist," when he is just the opposite. His genuine friendships with blacks extend back to his days in Hollis, when he didn't know there was supposed to be something unusual about that; they now cover a wide range of people, from shoe shine boys to distinguished educators.

At the University of Washington, the advance suspicions that Royal might have trouble with the blacks on the squad proved totally unwarranted. And then came that ridiculous fiasco in the Cotton Bowl, during the Syracuse game, when concerted efforts were made to apply racial overtones to a routine "Kill the referee!" rhubarb.

Royal, looking back from 13 years out, took a most charitable view of that situation—even though he felt the criticism was completely unjustified.

"I think they were after greater things when they blew that up as much as they could, and I don't blame 'em for doing that," he said. "I think if I'd been black, I'd have used just about any tactic I could to get an equal chance."

But he certainly would have stopped short of outright lies, he declared.

In January of 1970, the Associated Press carried an article claiming that Royal and four other head coaches from major colleges met with black coaches in Washington, D.C., on Jan. 12, 1970. The article, written by Bob Greene of the AP's Milwaukee Bureau, said the other major college coaches involved were John Pont of Indiana, Lloyd Eaton of Wyoming, Bear Bryant of Alabama and Cal Stoll of Wake Forest.

Royal was quoted as telling the black coaches, "You have not been publicized by your public relations people and the black coach has not reached the point where his coaching is as scientific as it is in the major colleges."

When he first heard of the article, Royal termed it a "vicious invention" that was completely false, and said he had not attended such a meeting. Furthermore, he declared, "Such things are not in my heart, and I could not have made those statements."

And he had a perfect alibi. At the time the AP claimed he was in Washington attending that meeting, Royal was in Austin accepting the AP national championship trophy from Mrs. Johnson at the Longhorn football banquet!

"That story was totally fabricated," Royal declared, several years later. "It was not connected to anything. It was not misrepresented—it was a total lie."

Shortly after it appeared, Royal contacted Louis Nizer, the famed New York attorney, about the possibility of suing for libel.

"He said he thought I had a good suit," said Royal. "He was interested in taking it but he said he wanted me to be prepared for a nasty situation. All I wanted was for the mess to be cleared up—and I wanted to keep on coaching. If I had been ready to get out of coaching, I would have taken 'em on. I felt like they really needed to be punished for that—and I still do, but it's too late now, of course.

"I think that went a long way toward hurting our recruiting of blacks. I think that could be proved to a jury—and also that this hurt me professionally. But the Associated Press ran an apology and I let it go at that, just because I didn't want to get involved in a nasty suit.

"You know, the people who really know me wonder how I could have the image I have for being against blacks—and I really do, too—but I just have to tell them that it's a long story . . . ."

Just as he was suspected at the University of Washington simply because he went there from Mississippi, Royal obviously has sustained some "racism" shots merely because he represents the University of Texas.

Royal's determination to avoid any appearance that he was trying to exploit or capitalize on his association with blacks has kept him, even in the face of ridiculous "racism" charges, from citing such things as the fact that Edith used to take a little blind, black youngster to football games and describe the action to him. Even now, Royal is reluctant to talk about such incidents.

"I just don't see what difference it makes what color anybody is," he said.

"I never have been anti-black and I've never mistreated any person, regardless of whether he was poor, or black, or whatever. I know how I've felt, ever since I was a kid, that these people were my friends. It was a natural, honest thing. But until a few years ago, I didn't express my concern about the inequities which existed. I was just unconcerned, and I feel badly now that I was.

"But as far as putting people down, or feeling they were inferior or minding being with them, that has never been the situation with me. I do think my attitude has changed because of education and maturity, and just looking around at what was right and what was wrong and what's fair. And I started looking around a lot more at these things after President Johnson and I became friends.

"I'm just appalled to think that, only a few years ago, we had state universities that weren't open to blacks—including the University of Texas. Isn't that a ridiculous thing, for a state university not to be open to blacks?"

He noted that the Heman Marion Sweatt case, which resulted in integration of the University of Texas, was not decided until 1950.

"That may seem like a long time ago," said Royal, "but isn't it ridiculous to think that, even in my lifetime, a guy couldn't attend a state university just because his skin was black? And then, even after they could get in school here, they had housing problems. Housing and eating facilities have been opened up to blacks since I came to Texas, in 1957. At that time, they couldn't even go in a campus cafeteria and eat. Now wasn't that ridiculous? They're students here but they can't go in a cafeteria.

"President Johnson opened up a big part of that, so that you could use a restroom, or go into a hotel, or go into a restaurant—go any place that you've got money enough to go into. He was really proud of that, and I think he should have been. I'm just glad that he got the satisfaction of seeing so many of his ideas along that line implemented."

Royal feels that, although great progress has been made in this field, much remains to be done. And the next step?

"Even now," he said, "there might be a little cringing when you walk into a restaurant and see a black over at the next table. What's next? For people not to be concerned whether others are black or brown or what they are, if they're in a restaurant. To accept 'em. Just looks—just a look on your face, whether you smile or whether you frown or whether you ignore them, makes a person feel uncomfortable or welcome or unwelcome. I don't know of any kind of law you can pass for that, but the change needs to come in all of us. I'm not any wide-eyed leader but my eyes have been opened up a lot as a result of being around President Johnson.

"I believe my thinking always was basically right, but it just never had been brought out before. I had tried to recruit blacks at the University of Texas. But the big thing always was the academic barrier, just because blacks had not had equal educational opportunities. That situation will gradually disappear, as more and more school systems are integrated and, hopefully, it will eventually be erased completely.

"Then we had to go through this thing where people claimed that blacks were not wanted at the University of Texas. The recruiters from other schools put this idea across. Texas is no more prejudiced and no less prejudiced than the other colleges and universities in Texas. No more, no less. Certainly, it's not the worst. But the recruiters from other schools make Texas the big villain when they're talking to blacks. As a result of that, I think a lot of blacks have turned their backs on a great opportunity at the University of Texas. And that's a discouraging fact, to think that they're not taking advantage of the opportunities at Texas, simply because other people are scaring them away from here.

"I think that's disappearing, and I think Roosevelt Leaks has had as much to do with it as anybody," said Royal. "Just through his performance. They see him doing well, they see him being accepted, they see his teammates slap him on the back after a good play.

"The publicity on Texas being 'racist' is beginning to melt and go away," he added, "and I think that's also true on some of the publicity about me being a racist."

That may be due, at least in part, to a five-article series on Royal's alleged racism which was carried by the AP the week before Texas played TCU in 1972. That brought the innuendoes and rumors to something of a climax. It also resulted in disclosures by Royal's friends of such facts as his service on the Board of Trustees for Stillman College, a Presbyterian school for blacks in Tuscaloosa, Alabama. That was one of the things Royal had kept quiet simply because he felt he might be accused of trying to exploit a cause about which he had deep feelings. Pressed for details about the school after his board service came to light, Royal talked enthusiastically about Stillman in general and about one of its programs in particular.

"They have about a hundred students there who don't really qualify for college, just because they don't have the background," he said. "The ability is there but it just hasn't been brought out. They'll take these kids and work with them until they're capable of passing entrance exams and going on to do college-level work. Those kids would be lost, otherwise. And Stillman is the only school I know of that has such a program for kids of that kind.

"The vast majority of students at Stillman are on some kind of scholarship," he added, "because they're poor kids."

Royal did not volunteer any information on his connection with Stillman, nor on his close friendships with several blacks, when Jack Keever and Robert Heard, of the AP's Austin Bureau, interviewed him for the series on his alleged racism and charges of prejudice in the UT Athletics Department. And they apparently did not discover such aspects of the matter from other sources.

With Royal's permission, they did interview the Longhorns' six black players—Leaks, Whittier, Donald Ealey, Howard Shaw, Lonnie Bennett and Fred Perry. At the time, Leaks, Whittier and Ealey all were in the starting lineup.

The mere fact that Texas had three blacks on the first team (when it had had none on the squad as recently as 1969) prompted some questions about the purpose and timing of the AP series. The fact that it appeared the week before the TCU game provoked more, especially from sports columnists throughout the state.

Maysel, in his *Austin American* column on Nov. 17, 1972, commented:

"There are indications that the AP writers approached it with the idea that the series would give an accurate picture of UT's and Royal's problem with a somewhat false anti-black image. However, it didn't all turn out as expected.

"The six black players, when interviewed together, spoke of a feeling of racism in Royal's program without offering any concrete evidence.

"And instead of weighing their words, being sure these represented their true feelings and realizing the wide circulation they would receive, they shot from the hip and let it all hang out.

"It's uncertain what the end result will be. Even though there has been a recanting of some of the most provocative statements, the damage has been done in some people's minds . . . ."

Leaks was quoted in the series as saying, "There's gonna be prejudice wherever you go to school." But Keever and Heard said he agreed with the other blacks that "there was racism among the Longhorn coaches" even though they could not give specific examples. And they reported that all the blacks except Ealey said they would come to Texas if they had it to do over.

After Ealey read the first article of the series, in *The Daily Texan* (the campus newspaper) on Monday morning, he became the first of the six players to go to Royal and say he was misunderstood.

"I just had to talk to him," Ealey said of his visit with Royal. "Oh, God, I had to explain. He was very understanding and he knew how I felt."

Ealey said his comments did not come out the way he intended them, even though he did not claim he had been misquoted.

"If I had it to do all over again, I wouldn't have said some of the things I said," declared Ealey, adding that he would recommend attending the University of Texas to anyone—and he was not sorry he had chosen it.

Whittier also wished he could have another chance. The interview took place in a "pressure situation," he said, "and we were trying to say what we wanted to say right off the top of our heads."

"If I had a chance to try again," said Whittier, "it would come out a lot different. My choice of words and things like that would be different."

The Royals' home was being remodeled at the time and they were living in an apartment near the campus. Finally, on Friday morning, Whittier went there and became the sixth of the black players to discuss the matter with Royal.

Whittier said he really had been trying to help but was "just clumsy."

"If you were trying to help, you really were clumsy," Royal told him. "You were clumsy as hell."

Whittier laughed.

"It looks kinda bad, doesn't it?" he asked.

"I thought it did," said Royal.

"Well, I just wanted to tell you I really don't feel that way," Whittier declared. "The way it came out was not the way I intended it."

"That's fine," said Royal. "It doesn't matter what interpretation anyone else puts on it, as long as you and I understand how we feel. That's all that really matters, anyway. So if you're all straight and you've got it off your chest, and you feel like we're ready to go play TCU, go on back to your work and forget it."

"I just wanted to come and talk to you about it," said Whittier.

"I'm glad you did," said Royal.

There was some speculation at the time that the "unity" and "teamwork" for which the Longhorns had gained unusual acclaim during the season might be destroyed by the AP series. In fact, some feared that the whites on the team might be especially upset by the statements from the blacks which appeared in the newspapers. But Texas whipped TCU, 27-0, and then clobbered Texas A&M, 38-3, before a nationwide television audience on a rainy Thanksgiving night in Memorial Stadium.

"Those players just said some things without thinking—some things they didn't mean," Royal said of the blacks' interview with AP. "They really didn't know what they were getting into. They got in there all together, and they're not going to say everything's just lovely here—or else

their own people would call 'em 'Uncle Toms.' Heard and Keever caught
Ealey when he was dejected by his football situation, not by the way he
was being treated . . . .

"I saw an interview with Roosevelt and Julius on television, on
Station KLRN, a little later and they did a much better job of expressing
themselves. In fact, they did a helluva job. They didn't say there was no
prejudice at the University of Texas—but they go ahead and say there is
prejudice everywhere.

"Julius said he thought Texas is more liberal-minded and more
open-armed than the other schools. 'But you ask me if there's prejudice at
Texas and you're backing in there where you make Texas look
bad'—that's the way Julius answered 'em on TV. That's not the way he'd
answered the Associated Press but he'd had time to back off and reflect
and think about it.

"I think Julius was baffled that I treated him the same way after that
AP series as I had before, and just the way I always had.

"Back at the start of the '72 season, he got offsides a couple of times
and I jumped him about it in a squad meeting. I told him, 'It's a lack of
poise—you're not delivering in a pressure situation.'

"Well, he came to see me later and takes it that I'm saying *blacks*
can't deliver under pressure. I said, 'Julius, are you trying to put a *black*
connotation on this, me correcting you?'

"He said, 'Well, I've wondered about it.' And I told him, 'You give
me another word for it; I say you don't have any *poise*. We get in a tight
situation and you can't hold 'til the third count. What word would you use
to describe it? I'll tell you one thing: being black is not going to keep you
from getting your ass chewed out. And being black is not going to keep
you from getting patted on the back.'"

Whittier thought a moment and then asked, "Well, have I lost my
position on the team?"

"No," Royal replied, "but the only reason you haven't is that I think
you're a better football player than the guy behind you. But I can tell you
this: you jump offsides a few more times and you're *not* a better football
player than he is. You keep losing your poise in tight situations and the
other guy, in my opinion, will be a better football player than you are. But
don't come in here and complain, every time I criticize you or correct you
for a mistake, that it's because you're black. I didn't jump offsides—you
did."

Whittier, a senior, dropped by Royal's office one day during the
spring of 1973, not long after Marian Royal Kazen had died, while Edith
was there—and said he would like to see her.

"She's in the next room," said Royal. "Go on back there."

"I just haven't seen her since you lost your daughter," said Whittier,
"and I want to visit with her."

As Whittier walked back to the conference room to see Edith, Royal praised him to a visitor who happened to be in his office at the time.

"That's awfully nice of Julius," he said. "He's been by to see me since we lost Marian but he hasn't seen Edith, and she's always thought a lot of him.

"And this is a far cry," he added, "from what a lot of people think the situation is around here."

The most stirring defense of Royal provoked by the AP series was Sports Editor Dan Cook's column in the Nov. 19, 1972, issue of the *San Antonio Express-News*. It appeared under the headline, "Royal Got Bad Rap In AP Series" with a subhead, "Five Parts of Factless Prose," and is reproduced here with permission:

> *The five-part Associated Press series on Darrell Royal and possible racism in the University of Texas athletic department has now been completed and one of the world's largest wire services stands responsible for one of the most factless character assassinations in modern journalism history.*
>
> *Many thousands of words were used in the lengthy series but never at any time did the authors produce a single shred of evidence to insinuate that the Texas coach might, indeed, be a racist.*
>
> *Instead, Jack Keever and Robert Heard of the Associated Press' Austin bureau relied on innuendo, hear-say and quotes from several black players who told how they "had nothing to put their fingers on but they could just sense that Royal is a racist."*
>
> *The second part of the series gave the true tone of the authors' work as they opened with the following statement: "Darrell Royal's image is so bad among some blacks that they suspect he even taunts and mistreats his maid."*
>
> *That's like writing, "The Associated Press' image is so bad in Austin some readers suspect that they make up the news in Scholz' Beer Garden and deliver it on weekends."*
>
> *The very timing of the series is suspect, to say the least, since it wasn't prompted by a player demotion, a rebellion or even the slightest disturbance. Nor was it requested by anyone. Such "in-depth" type series usually run during the off-season and rarely if ever in the stretch of a hot campaign.*
>
> *It's even more surprising that the Associated Press, usually a rather conservative and cautious outfit, would attempt to tackle Coach Royal on this same subject so soon after inviting a libel case.*
>
> *That came early in 1970 when an AP story out of Washington told the world about a meeting Royal attended with some of the nation's top black coaches. Royal was quoted as making some derogatory remarks about the blacks' chances of ever coaching major white teams. The black coaches were quoted too. But there was no such meeting. As a matter of fact, at the time of that alleged meeting in Washington Royal*

was in Austin receiving the Associated Press national championship trophy from Mrs. Lyndon B. Johnson.

The recent Associated Press series did not run in the Express or News. I made that decision after reading the first two parts. But it did run in many other papers across this state.

It ran in the San Antonio Light where it was well displayed with such damaging headlines as "Darrell Royal Struggling to Shed Racist Image." And, "Racism Among Texas Coaches, Say UT Athletes."

It's a bad sick rap for Royal, who seems to be caught up in one of the hottest witch hunts since Senator McCarthy went looking for commies.

So many claim to know Royal so well. Yet so few really know the man at all. The two AP writers who handled the series have visited the coach many times but they've never made any real effort to uncover any facts about his true feelings regarding racism. Instead they labored long and hard on the other side of the fence and still came up empty-handed. They had to settle for innuendoes.

The AP writers didn't bother to check with the first black star Royal ever coached for a true test of his feelings during the early stages of the coach's career. That would be Rollie Miles, one of three black starters on Royal's Edmonton Eskimo team in the old Canadian League.

Tom Stolhandske, county commissioner here, played under Darrell on that same pro team and he recalls only too well how Royal, then just 28, called several white players aside and chewed on them for talking bigotry. Stolhandske remembers how the youthful Darrell and Edith Royal often entertained black players at home and just as often visited their homes. There were no social barriers and he, Stolhandske, a young man from Baytown, Texas, was impressed with the easy, fine feeling that prevailed.

It might be safe to assume that the AP writers never heard of Harry Wilson, a Killeen high school player who was injured in a game a few years back. Royal didn't know him either when he visited Harry at a Temple clinic many times. Darrell just knew that the kid would never walk again and he was in bad shape. Royal thought a visit from him might lift the boy's spirits just a bit. He wasn't surprised to learn that Harry is black but he was depressed to learn how desperate the Wilson family was for financial assistance. That's why he gave $500 out of his pocket to the family of that youngster.

And that's the only reason he gave it. Only one other person knew of it but when I heard the story months later I was warned if I ever told it or printed it Royal would be furious. So be it.

Some might say that Royal offers such "little gestures" toward blacks in the hope that someday those deeds will be discovered. If that is the case the writers who visit him so often are slow reaching the areas of discovery and Royal himself offers no hints or help. But for those who still believe that way—this, then, is the day of revelation.

The black people in Tuscaloosa, Alabama are sure going to be surprised when they hear that "so many" Texans figure Royal is a racist. It's not well known here but for the past three years Darrell has been on the board of trustees of Stillman University, a black school in Tuscaloosa.

But Mexican-Americans might be happy to hear that his hang-up is mostly with blacks. Especially Mexican-Americans attending Pan American in Kingsville, the prep school for students having trouble with English but eager to attend college. Royal has served on the board of trustees of that Presbyterian school for four years.

And Charley Pride, the first black country and western singer to make it big, will be shocked to hear of Royal's problems concerning racism. Mr. and Mrs. Pride went on vacation with Mr. and Mrs. Royal to Jamaica this year and both couples had one of the finest times of their lives.

That, however, really isn't worth passing along to the AP and others. After all, Royal probably wouldn't have gone with Pride had he not been a famous singer and guitar picker. And by the same token, Pride might not have gone with Royal had he not been a famed football coach.

Both couples would have missed a lot of fun and a fine friendship had not the two men risen to the peaks of their profession. As a matter of fact, were it not for their special talents, Pride might still be picking cotton in Sledge, Mississippi and Royal might still be shining shoes in Hollis, Okla.

Come to think of it, that could lead us to the only real racist act of Royal's life. He was the only white shoeshine boy in Hollis throughout his high school days, thus knocking some black kid out of a job. But the black shine boys didn't seem to resent him because they gave pointers on the best way to get a high, glossy shine.

Looking back on that series, you wonder just how much checking and effort the two AP writers really put to their task. It's frightening to consider how a man like Royal could become the subject for a five-part series, the target of racist charges.

The moods of our time are unpredictable and forever changing in swift and sometimes sad strokes. It's particularly sad that two staff writers for such a large, responsible unit of communication would be given such a free, reckless hand.

And it's even more distressing that so many newspapers would choose to publish such factless prose. But then, perhaps there's some comfort to be found in the fact that editors still have a choice on using such material.

Royal said Heard and Keever told him before they wrote the series that they were trying to help.

"I do think they had good intentions," Royal declared later. "They printed what they got. They talked to me about doing the story and I said, 'fine.' I didn't want to tell them they couldn't do it, partly because it might look like I was trying to cover up something.

"And I also figured that if these guys are on the squad and they've seen me, and worked with me—and if they can't endorse me, there must be something wrong with me. But I think it came out entirely—well, it just doesn't express their views. I think you could go back and interview 'em now and it would be entirely different."

Still, Royal and his close friends remain baffled by the totally false image created of him through such incidents as the Syracuse game rhubarb, the AP's false story on the Washington meeting of coaches, and the AP series.

"I'm just tired of trying to defend it," Royal said of his reputation on race relations. "I'm just going to go by my record and my deeds and my thoughts and, eventually, the record is going to be tallied up. I'm going to do what I think is right and do the very best job I can and, in the end, I think it will be tallied up right.

"But in the meantime, I guess I'm just not going to be able to convince people that I don't beat my wife and I don't kick blacks."

Still the best of friends are Royal and Earl Campbell, one of the greatest running backs in UT history. They have tremendous respect for each other.

Chapter 19

WINNER OF DISCONTENT

A few days before the AP series appeared, a book entitled *Meat on the Hoof* (St. Martin's Press, New York) showed up in the bookstores. It was written by Gary Shaw, a reserve guard on the Longhorn squad during the years 1963-1967. It painted a brutal, almost sadistic picture of college football, especially at the University of Texas, and depicted Royal as a coach who would do just about anything to win.

Shaw's most serious charge probably was that Royal authorized Trainer Frank Medina and the assistant coaches to put mediocre players through cruel, punishing drills designed to run them off and thus make their athletic scholarships available for others. But Shaw also complained that Lan Hewlett, the academic counselor for athletes (popularly known as the "brain coach"), arranged tutoring for good players and helped them get "crip" courses but refused to help the marginal ones. He also claimed that it was difficult for poor players to get medical treatment when they were injured.

It should be noted that Shaw mentions in his own book that, three years after he left the Longhorn football squad, he voluntarily sought psychiatric treatment.

When Royal showed up for his weekly meeting with the Longhorn Club on Wednesday, Nov. 15, 1972, he brought up the Shaw book and the AP series on his own.

"It looks like we've got a lot of problems," he declared. "I used to really get concerned about things like that, but the older I get, the more I feel like just telling 'em to kiss my ass! I'm not real concerned. I would be if I felt these things represented a consensus opinion. In fact, if I felt that way, I'd just set my bucket down. I don't know any other way to run our program except to try and be fair and honest and win, within the bounds of ethics."

He noted that all coaches have plenty of critics.

"Any time you have somebody sitting on the bench," he said, "you've got a potential family of enemies."

Elaborating on that observation in an interview, Royal said a coach's own bench can easily produce about 100 enemies a year.

"You play twenty-two men and you've got another thirty-five or forty sitting on the bench," he explained. "Those people on the bench know they should be playing, and they've got their girl friends convinced of it. Their parents and friends and relatives all know those guys are better than the ones on the field, and they blame the coach for playing the wrong ones. So it's easy for a coach to create a hundred or so enemies every year."

Several months later, in response to questions, Royal charitably recalled Shaw as one who "gave a good effort in football and did well in his studies." And, although Royal said he had not read Shaw's book, he answered several specific questions raised by it.

"We've got to have a central point the players go through when they're going to see those doctors," he declared. "We can't just turn one hundred and fifteen guys loose and let them go see whoever they want to, especially when we're paying for it. They go for colds, flu, all sorts of things. We have to have some kind of control over it. They can go see a doctor any time they want to—but if they want us to pay for it, we tell 'em to clear it with us so we'll know what's going on. That's all. It's just that simple. Anytime someone else is paying your medical bills, you've got channels you go through and procedures you have to follow. They don't just turn you loose.

"And as for scholarships, I've never been limited on them. I've tried to get the drones out, but any efficient organization does that. We've got lots of guys who played less than Shaw, who were out there on their own, who don't feel like we tried to get rid of them. There have been a lot of guys here with lesser ability who don't feel the way he does. That's just one guy's opinion.

"Shaw says he took some psychiatric treatment while he was here. That's kind of common these days—but I never have felt the need to go take treatment.

"Shaw's one of those guys that wants everybody to love everybody, and for everybody to be treated alike. I think that would be great, but this ol' world just doesn't turn that way. Winning football coaches are not treated the same way as losing football coaches. Good writers are not treated the same way as sorry writers. That's just the way the system is.

"Now, as far as mistreating players because they don't have ability, that's bull. We don't mistreat or abuse anybody. Shaw certainly didn't have any reason to complain. He said he had some physical problems and wanted to quit football; finally, we just let him drop out of football and keep his scholarship. I don't know what he's bitching about."

Royal admits that college football is not perfect but insists that you cannot change an entire program to fit two or three players. And he contends that the main difference between today's football players and those of 20 years ago is simply that "more of 'em write books today."

As for discipline, Royal is a strong believer in it—but with a minimum of rules.

"I expect the players to be on time at meetings and practices, and go all out in practice, and do their best to be good representatives of the University of Texas," he declared. "I don't want eighty guys waiting on one when we start to go on a trip, for instance.

"I don't have any set punishment for violations, because I think you should deal with each case individually—and how you deal with each one depends on the circumstances involved and the boy's attitude. You have to have some type of guidelines. But without our laying down any hard and fast rules, these players know right from wrong.

"It doesn't take any Einstein to know you're supposed to be on time—that if practice starts at three-thirty, you're supposed to be on the field at three-thirty. I don't think they're confused as to what's expected of them.

"When I first came here, we used to say that a guy who cut class had to run up and down the stadium a certain number of times. It sounded like a good idea, but it didn't work; you just can't make blanket rules like that to fit everyone.

"We soon found out that those who were lying to me about it were getting by with cutting classes, because some of the profs didn't think attendance was that important and wouldn't give us an attendance record. In a case like that, all you're doing is encouraging a kid to lie to you," said Royal.

"If an honor student wants to cut a class, I think he knows what he's doing and he ought not to have to run the stadium because of it. But then, how am I going to separate him from someone who is not doing well academically and really needs to attend every class? So the main thing we try to do now is to make them *want* to attend their classes and do well in their studies.

"We also had compulsory study hall at first, but we did away with that because you can lead a cow to water but you can't make her drink. And some of the players would put off studying during the day because they knew they'd be in study hall at night. It's better for them to learn to handle their own affairs.

"Athletics is one of the last strongholds of discipline—and there's been a strong pecking away at that, by the element that wants to see the establishment fall completely. But this will be the last place they'll penetrate and destroy.

"Our squad members are told all the time what fools they are to listen to us, and adhere to all these 'unrealistic' rules they have to obey in order to play football. They get this put on them constantly by some of the other students, who ask why they put up with all these restrictions.

"And then Dr. John Silber leaves our faculty and goes to Boston University, and advocates that coaches be required to sit up in the grandstands during football games. He says he resents my being out there with a headset telling the players what to do during their 'final exams.'

"A lot of people outside athletics just can't understand athletics. They don't understand what this 'hold' is that you can maintain over athletes and get them to move as a unit," said Royal. "I couldn't explain it to them. I know it's important to me and it's important to these players. I think the players feel that what they are doing is right and is worthwhile, and is worth the sacrifices they're making. And that's really all I'm concerned about. I'm not concerned about trying to convince some of these other people, on the outside."

Among the players who came away "convinced" was Gene Bledsoe, a three-year starter whose views were diametrically opposed to those of Shaw. But he and Shaw were good friends, and Shaw devoted a chapter of his book to Bledsoe.

That prompted Bledsoe to write a letter, dated January 9, 1973, to Royal. Some excerpts from that letter:

Dear Coach:

Because of the vast differences between my opinions and those stated by Gary Shaw in Meat on the Hoof, I feel compelled to express my views of the University of Texas football program and its head coach.

I spent many hours talking with Gary while he was researching his book. After these discussions I thought I had a good idea as to the proposed content of the book. I was mistaken. I read the book when it first came out and was impressed with Gary's writing ability and narrative; however, I could not believe he was writing about the same school which I attended. As you know, Gary and I were friends while at the University, and we have remained friends. Nevertheless, the fact that two people at the same place and time could have had experiences so totally different is beyond my comprehension.

My four years at the University were some of the most pleasant and enjoyable of my life. They were certainly the most beneficial and rewarding. I received an outstanding education, was privileged to participate in one of the finest football programs in the country—directed by the finest coach. The importance of these statements, however, is not the separate assertions that the University provides a superior education, or wins football games, or even that Darrell Royal is a quality coach. The importance is the interaction of these three ingredients . . . .

Contrary to Gary's accusations, I have always been impressed by the honesty and frankness that permeates you and your program at Texas. In fact, my reason for even attending the University of Texas was precipitated by your frank honesty. Gary also speaks of your inaccessibility to players and your coolness to them off the field. This accusation I must likewise refute. On occasions I had problems which I felt needed your personal attention. You always met me warmly and gave immediate consideration to these problems. I know of absolutely no athlete who was refused your individual attention when openly sought. I remember the interest displayed by you in all aspects of our life at Texas.

I was repeatedly amazed by your knowledge and visible concern for all the Texas 'student-athletes.' One personal example occurred when I jokingly mentioned my girl's dismay at my position being called 'weak tackle.' Shortly thereafter, the 'weak side' linemen began being called 'quick side' linemen.

I sorely regret that Meat on the Hoof will be read and believed by many people. Accusations, such as doctors were not easily accessible to every player, will be believed; when, in fact, there were doctors at nearly every practice, and in the dressing room after practice . . . .

I was amazed at Gary's implication that your only interest in an athlete's education was in his scholastic eligibility—not in his learning. However, for me and many others who never had trouble just passing courses, the free assistance of qualified tutors made an invaluable contribution to a quality education.

While on the subject of education, Gary says that punishment for 'cutting' classes was assessed differently for starters than for the other players. Well, he may have been right, for I also participated in the episode of 'running the stands' he describes in his book. I was required to run thirty trips in comparison to Gary's twenty; both of us had only one cut.

. . . I consider the image portrayed of you and the University of Texas football program in Gary's book as grossly exaggerated, distorted, and totally slanted.

Coach, you were a hard task-master and always demanded a great deal from all those around you. However, as time has disassociated me with mostly a football life and associated me with other aspects of life. I realize that you demanded no more of me then than I should demand of myself. . . .

> *Sincerely,*
> */s/ Gene Bledsoe*
> *Gene Bledsoe*

Among the many other unsolicited letters Royal received from former players as a result of the book was this one from Marvin T. Kubin, a 1960-61-62 letterman, dated June 27, 1973:

Dear Coach Royal,

You have undoubtedly received many letters and have been asked many questions about the book Meat on the Hoof, so I will not bother you with questions regarding something that, in my opinion, was written by someone with such untrue and exaggerated ideas.

The book did make me stop and do some thinking which prompted this letter. I don't remember ever thanking you for all that you did for me while I was at the University of Texas. I want to thank you at this time for showing concern for me at a time when I had nothing to offer you and you were doing all the offering. The time I am referring to is when I had just flunked out of school and you were willing to help me get another scholarship elsewhere. As it turned out, I wanted another chance to stay at Texas and you gave me that chance. To me, this is a quality in you I find completely contrary to what Mr. Shaw attempts to describe.

I do not know what my life would have been like without you, football and the University of Texas, but I do feel that knowing you and having played football has played a great part in getting me where I am today. The main thing that has stuck in my mind through the years is when you told me, "If a man's goals are too low he will never surpass them." My goals are so high that I may never achieve them but each time I climb a rung I feel I owe you a big portion of the thanks.

This "Thank You" is long overdue, but I did want you to know how this former athlete of yours feels, and I hope someday my son can play for you.

> *Sincerely,*
> */s/ Marvin T. Kubin*
> *Marvin T. Kubin*

Someone who read Shaw's book told Royal it contained three chapters devoted to the emphasis the Longhorn coach puts on winning, and saying it is of paramount importance to him.

"If he said that, he's damned sure got that part right," said Royal, "because I want everybody around here wanting to win. If there's anybody around here who doesn't want to win, I want 'em to get gone. That goes for the team, the coaches, the secretaries, the janitors—anybody. I want 'em all wanting to win. So he sure as hell had that right! But he was around here long enough to know that we always stay within the rules and within the bounds of ethics."

Chapter 20

HIT AND MYTH

When someone introduced Royal and Mickey Mantle to each other at a Cotton Bowl party a few years ago, Royal was delighted and told Mantle how happy he was to meet him.

"We have so many mutual friends," said Royal, "and they've told me so much about you that I'm glad we finally got a chance to meet."

Mantle stood there, grinning, during that brief monologue and then replied, "We've met before."

"Oh, I don't think so," said Royal, with a puzzled look on his face. "I'm sure I'd remember it if we had. Are you sure?"

"Yes," said the former New York Yankee star. "It was in 1949, when I graduated from high school and visited the Oklahoma campus as a football prospect. You showed me around up there."

"Oh," said Royal. He thought a moment and then added, "But you weren't *Mickey Mantle* then!"

In a way, it's surprising that Royal would think of expressing that particular thought that way because, in his own mind, *he* always has been and always will be just Darrell Royal. And he seems to take pride in being his "natural self," despite the honors and accolades which have been heaped upon him as he walked with presidents but kept the common touch.

He didn't mind being identified as a country-western music fan even before country-western music became fashionable. As a matter of fact, he says he has loved that kind of music ever since the 1930s, when Dr. John R. Brinkley was selling goat glands on a Del Rio radio station which reached all the way to Hollis—at least after dark. And in those days, Royal enjoyed listening at noon to the "Light Crust Doughboys," who were featured on a Fort Worth station and who helped W. Lee O'Daniel, their announcer, win the Texas governor's race in 1938.

As a youngster then, Royal could not stretch even his wildest and most ambitious dreams to the point of thinking he would ever be visiting a President of the United States in the White House living quarters. Or riding around the President's ranch with him in a Lincoln convertible, then vacationing with him in Acapulco. Or having Gregory Peck give him a personal tour of Hollywood, or having Bob Hope become a personal friend. Or vacationing with Charley Pride.

W. L. Todd, Royal, Bob Hope and Arnold Palmer get together at the Byron Nelson Classic in Dallas on April 29, 1970.

(Photo by Bob Jackson)

"It still baffles and amazes me," Royal said after becoming one of the most famous football coaches in the country, "when I reflect on what's happened to me and the people I've met."

Father Bomar, who has spent a great deal of time with Royal during recent years, describes him as a "very gentle, highly sensitive, unselfish and uncomplicated man who is one of the most honest people I know."

Father Bomar recalls that, in December of 1969, as he and Royal were driving back to Austin after a visit with Steinmark at the M. D. Anderson Hospital, he brought up the subject of Royal's rumored retirement from coaching.

"I told him I knew he didn't need my advice, that he had plenty of counsel within himself," said Father Bomar, "but I hoped he would reconsider and not discontinue coaching. I felt he had much to contribute to the sport, and I felt collegiate football was in a critical stage, and might not survive. And I told him I thought he had much more to contribute than anybody I knew of.

"Darrell said he *had* thought of quitting, after winning the national championship that year, but he had decided that was a selfish thing for him to even think about. He said he had reconsidered and was going to keep on.

"Darrell is aggressive, he's impatient, he's a winner, and I doubt that he would be happy doing anything else. He loves young people and he likes to be around them. He likes their spirit, their enthusiasm and their energy. And he likes to watch them. But sometimes, of course, their troubles make him awfully sad.

"I remember the day before Christmas Eve in 1971, when we drove to Temple to see Harry Wilson, the high school player who had broken his neck. It was a beautiful, sunshiny day and Darrell said, 'Boy, I sure would like to be out playing golf today.' But then he thought a moment and said, 'But I'd sure rather be driving up here to see that boy than lying in a hospital bed myself without being able to see anything but the ceiling.'"

Royal's feeling that to quit coaching, after reaching the pinnacle of success, would be "selfish" indicated that his feelings had gone full circle.

"When I got into coaching, it was a selfish thing," he declared. "I got into it because it was fun for me and it was what I wanted to do. Sure, I'd heard about all the good that athletics did for people; but, frankly, that's not the reason I got into coaching."

Now, he felt he could make a continuing contribution and that it would be somewhat selfish on his part to quit. But, he added firmly, he would not stay in coaching "two minutes if it ever got to the point where I was not at the controls."

"You can't take over the controls and *force* people to do things," Royal said. "That's one of the main tricks in coaching. You have to make people *want* to do things because they want to win. But one guy has to handle the controls. The players have to be trained to respond when a decision is made. I don't have time to have a staff meeting on the sidelines to vote on a decision, or poll the squad on it. I have to make a decision within a few seconds on what we're going to do."

Royal feels that football, despite all the "team effort" required, still revolves around individuals.

"Most of my own motivation as a player came from wanting to do my personal job well," he declared. "I think I had enough pride to want to play my position well—to play it better than the guy on the other side was playing the same position.

"I don't think anyone ever had to get me ready to play football. And I think that basically, although a coach can guide it some, a team has to get ready as individuals. That's always been my approach to it.

"You talk about *team effort.* What is team effort? Team effort is getting a bunch of individuals ready to play, and then the team plays enthusiastically. But you still have to go back to the individual.

"A big percentage of it is mental," said Royal. "Football is not a natural game. *What's natural about two guys backing off and running into each other?* That's not natural. It's a totally *unnatural* game. Linemen getting down and playing in an ape-like position, for instance, playing low—we're built to walk upright; we're built to maneuver and get about in an *upright* position. We're not built to get down and play like linemen; that's not natural.

"There's *nothing* natural about football. You go down and watch people Christmas-shopping. They'll have an occasional bump but they very carefully try to *avoid* each other. That's the *natural* thing to do. As they walk along the crowded sidewalks, they try the best they can to dodge each other because they don't like to run into other people. It hurts and it bruises.

"So how *unnatural* is it for guys in football to back off and run into each other at high speeds? There's *nothing* natural about that. And there wasn't anything natural about those Japs flying down those smokestacks, either. That's all mental. You've got to have people 'psyched up' to do that.

"Football is all psychological and emotional. You have to gear yourself up at a fanatical pitch in order to play football. And when you don't do that, the contact bruises and hurts more. You'll throw your head aside and play on the edges instead of getting right in the middle of it.

"When you're really ready, when that adrenalin is flowing and you're really keyed up, you don't even feel the contact. I didn't, when I was playing. But you go out to practice and you're not ready and you play around the edges, and everything hurts—every lick you get. When I'd get all geared up to play in a football game, I'd find bumps and bruises the next morning I didn't even know I had. And when I got 'em, I didn't even feel 'em.

"I know this sounds barbaric to a lot of the mommas," said Royal, "and a lot of the people who endorse the game of football don't go along with my thinking. But I think I'm just being more truthful about it than some people want to admit.

"You don't run into people unless you're geared up. You have to get 'psyched' up to run into people and knock folks around enough to come out on the long end of the score. That's the reason you can't scrimmage every day. If people really enjoyed doing this, you'd go out and scrimmage every day. But they really *don't* enjoy it.

"So why do they do it? For recognition. That's the only reason a guy plays football," said Royal.

"You'll hear a guy say, 'I just love to hit.' No, he doesn't just *love* to hit. He hits because it gains him recognition. If you think he just loves to hit, throw him some pads out there and say, 'Okay, Buster, you and that other guy who just loves to hit can go out there and run into each other, and hit all you want to, and nobody will ever know about it. They won't write about it, they won't put your pictures in the paper, they won't put it on television, and nobody will talk about it over coffee.'

"Then just let 'em go out there and see how long they hit each other. No, they don't *love* to hit. A guy would have to be a stone idiot to love going out there and just running into someone else. The reason they do go out there and run into each other is the recognition which results, not only for them as individuals but also for their team, their school or their home town.

"Even though a guy really participates in sports selfishly, the team element is there. At some stage, he must be willing to sacrifice individual glory for the good of the team—or else he's a misfit. And yet, any coach who thinks he can get any player to *continually* sacrifice individual attention for the good of the team is foolish. It's a give-and-take situation, and you have to maintain a balance. You can't get away from the team, and unity, but you can't get away, either, from the fact that individual recognition is extremely important.

"If guys didn't play for recognition, you could give 'em nice sports coats at the end of the season instead of letter jackets. They wouldn't stand still for *that* five minutes. Because that letter jacket is a badge of honor. They're proud of it, and they ought to be. Our players just love to show off those national championship rings—and who can blame them?

"This is all kind of a 'show biz' thing. Athletes are 'hams,' just as much as entertainers are—and so are coaches.

"Football is an emotional, psychological thing, and it's mental. It's an unnatural game that you've got to pep yourself up for.

"But I certainly don't think it's bad. I don't think it's bad to fight for a cause, or to fight for a reason—to be a winner, and to make sacrifices to be a winner.

"I couldn't care less what motivates a guy. People say it's wrong for boys to go to college just to play football; but if football causes a boy to go to class and causes him to study enough to pass his exams, I don't care what motivated him to get his education. I don't care what the carrot is out there, dangling, that pushes a guy beyond the limits that other people are willing to go, so long as the motivation, the drive, the incentive is there.

"I think you have to make some sacrifices for anything worthwhile—to write a good story, to sing a good song, to play a good football game, to teach a good class, to perform a good operation. To do any of these things you have to prepare. And even after you're prepared, you can't stay out all night the night before and expect to do a good job. Maybe you have to break away from that party a little early if you've got something important to do the next day, and you're a dedicated person.

"You've got to make sacrifices to excel in any field. Whatever you do, I think all the sacrifices and self-denials make you a stronger person. And that's certainly true of football. I definitely think it has a 'carry-over' value, although I'm *not* a 'compare-football-to-life' advocate.

"But it's there. There comes a time when you've got to sacrifice individual glory for the overall success of the team. And that's good for you. You've got to backtrack somewhere along the line for the good of other people. You can't be totally selfish all the way through.

"There are all sorts of levels of success in football—all-conference, first team, All-America, Heisman Trophy, second team, earn a letter, suit up. Some guys like to wear merthiolate and put on a bandage just to show they're out for football. But there are many different rungs on the ladder and that's the reason these young men make sacrifices, to climb that ladder—and I don't think that's bad."

Royal doesn't believe the basic situation has changed any at all during the years he has been interested in football.

"I've never talked about it with other coaches," he said. "Everybody has to be himself and coach his own way. You hear other people talk about 'teamwork' and 'character-building'—and I can buy all that, to a degree. But I also think it's more personal than that. I think that if you use the team approach too much, for instance, a player can use that as a dodge. He can say the team wasn't ready. But you can't dodge behind that, really, any more than if you're successful, you can walk in there and claim, 'I did it alone.'

"I hate a braggart. But victory has got to be a deep personal satisfaction to anybody that participated in it and had a hand in it. All the glory can't be heaped just on the team. The personal, individual aspect has to come in there.

"I say football doesn't build character," Royal declared, "and it shocks a lot of people to hear me say that. But I don't think it '*builds*' character. Football is a process that eliminates the *weak* of character while making those with *real* character even stronger. It's a case of the weak getting weaker and the strong getting stronger.

"When you come along and have a championship team, you've eliminated the weak of character and you've got the cream of the crop left, and you say, 'Look what *we* built!' But what you've really done is eliminate everybody who was weak. The ones who are left had strong character and dedication when they came here. But you didn't 'build' that—their mommas and daddies *built* it.

"I often tell parents, 'If you send me a good one, I'll send you a good one back. But if you send me a weak one, I'll probably return a weak one.' I don't take credit for the strong *character* of our championship teams; the mommas and daddies deserve that credit.But neither do I want to be blamed for some player who comes in here lighter than a June frost and can't stand the competition.

"If a dog is gonna bite you, he'll bite you as a puppy. If he's a striker and a fighter and a competitor, he was born that way. And a true winner has fought it all the way through, rising above his competitors. That's true in any field; if you're going to be successful, you've got to compete.

"So any time you teach people to compete—whether it's in football, or debate, or band, or swimming, or whatever it is—I think that's good.

"Football is just one area in which we compete. It gives character a chance to come to the front, and it gives people a chance to use their character and develop it. But a guy has to have the basic qualities, the basic character, before he starts. It's the job of a coach to feed character and strengthen it and keep it going, so that it has a chance to grow and develop."

Royal, who feels he owes a deep personal debt of gratitude to football, also believes that star athletes should provide some inspiration for youngsters when it comes to developing character. On that point, he disagreed strongly with a statement made by the New York Jets' Joe Namath, whom Royal considers a good friend and a "warm, sincere person with the best of manners."

"I think there's a lot *to* Joe," said Royal, "and I think he regrets somewhat the image he has. He's not a cocky, conceited guy—but he's not totally modest, either. He has a good balance. But I think he was wrong when he said he had no obligation to youth. I disagree violently with that. I feel he does have an obligation, whether he likes it or whether he doesn't. He's a national figure, a celebrity; he's looked up to, and he has an influence. He has an input, either plus or minus—and it's a case of which way he wants the input to be.

"I think that, now that he's getting a little older and more mature, he feels that he was a little bit wrong in saying that. And when he gets even older, he's going to see that it was *damned* wrong. I think he's a good enough person to make that adjustment. He was just a young kid and, in my opinion, he didn't handle that particular part of his career very well.

But I don't think he would intentionally hurt anyone and I still don't believe that's the way he really felt."

Since Namath came from a poor family in the coal fields of Pennsylvania, the one-time shoe shine boy from Hollis feels he has much in common with him. And he believes that Namath should be just as willing as he is to acknowledge his debt to college football.

"I think college football makes the strong stronger," said Royal. "It hones up and makes sharper a competitive edge that must be there to start with."

And it provides many other benefits, even for those who do not participate in it directly, he feels.

"It gives a release to the student body, in high school or college," he said. "We've had a restless age, and the kids are more expressive now. They're going to express themselves, one way or another. We have about thirty thousand University of Texas students who come to watch every home game—and this gives them a chance to let off steam. I think you'll find that we have fewer demonstrations, and less conflict, on the campus during the football season than at any other time. Our campus *needs* something like football.

"Football also helps to keep people interested in the University, and in the educational process—which really is a lot more important than football. I recognize that and admit it. But they schedule a lot of alumni meetings, for instance, around football games; a lot of people need football to keep them interested in the more important things.

"For the players it's meant for, college football is great," Royal declared, "but it's not meant for everyone. This old thing that if a guy gives up or quits football, he's yellow, is a bunch of hogwash.

"Football is just one test of courage. There are a lot of other tests of courage that a tough, aggressive football player would flunk. I long since have stopped saying that a guy who doesn't have the heart to play football is yellow, or non-courageous.

"Personally, I happen to detest going under water. I don't like to dive, or even jump, into a swimming pool; I just don't like to get my head under water—I guess maybe because I'm scared to. But I don't want anyone telling me I'm 'yellow' because I don't go out for the swimming team.

"Football is not meant for everyone. Everyone's not geared up for football. But for those who are geared up for football, thank goodness there's a game like football for them to play."

EPILOGUE

On December 4, 1976, Darrell Royal's Texas Longhorns defeated the Arkansas Razorbacks, 29–12, in Austin's Memorial Stadium — and then carried him off the field on their shoulders. Moments later, in the locker room, he shocked the football world by announcing that he was resigning as head football coach but would retain his position as director of athletics at the University of Texas.

Thus ended an era of unparalleled success in Southwest Conference coaching. During his 20 years at Texas, he won three national championships (1963, 1969, 1970) and won or shared 11 Southwest Conference titles. His record at Texas included 167 victories, 47 losses and five ties. He finished his career as one of the three top winning coaches of all time, with an overall record of 184–60–5. In 16 bowl appearances, his teams won eight, lost seven and tied one. In 23 years as a head coach, he never suffered a losing season.

"I'm not tired of coaching," he declared when he resigned, "but I wanted to get out before I got tired of it. I always wanted to leave somebody's house before they wanted me to leave."

He has never regretted his decision. And he has never had time to get even slightly bored. He continued to serve as director of athletics for three years and ever since has been a special assistant on athletics to the UT president.

He spends much of his time organizing and promoting golf and country music charity events. He is especially proud of his work with the East Austin Youth Classic, a celebrity golf tournament which has raised many thousands of dollars for disadvantaged youngsters. He also serves as chairman of the Board of Governors for the Barton Creek Country Club, which has three golf courses just a few miles from Austin.

"Things have fallen into place for me better than I could ever have dreamed," he said. "It seems that something has always fallen into place for me when I needed it. I've enjoyed every single phase of my life — except for the Depression and World War II."

As for the years since he left coaching, he sums them up without hesitation by declaring: "They've been great!"